At the Feet of an Avadhut

Life Lessons Learned Serving
Sri Kaleshwar

At the Feet of an Avadhut

Life Lessons Learned Serving
Sri Kaleshwar

By Terry 'Sundaram' Clark
with Jessica 'Sivapriya' Godino

With an Introduction by
Mataji

Published by

DIVINE MOTHER CENTER
Divine Mother Center
Laytonville, CA, USA

DEDICATION

We dedicate this book to our master, Sri Kaleshwar.

We want to thank Mataji, the Board Members and residents

of the Divine Mother Center,

and the students of our live satsang at the Virtual Ashram.

This book would not have come into the creation

without your love and support.

Ganesh Temple, Divine Mother Center

Shirdi Sai Baba

CONTENTS

PREFACE

by Terry 'Sundaram' Clark & Sivapriya Godino

Terry 'Sundaram' Clark:

I was Sri Kaleshwar's (Swami's) personal attendant for eleven years in India. I spent thousands of hours with him, and during that time he asked me numerous times to tell the truth about him and his life. He felt strongly about this. He asked me to tell what I had seen and experienced with him. He said that everything that happened needed to be written down, so people can know what it's like to be around an *avadhut*[1].

Most people don't have any idea of what an avadhut is, but the world really needs to know. An avadhut is a being who lives in the highest state of consciousness. Avadhuts are incomprehensible to the limited mind, their actions are inscrutable and misunderstood. They operate from beyond the mind, from universal consciousness. They live and operate from oneness. Avadhuts are the greatest blessing for humanity. A person in avadhut consciousness can change the world, like *Shirdi Baba*[2] and *Bhagawan Nityananda*[3].

Swami never taught me directly about this, but I must have gotten something right because he kept me close to him for all those years. When I came to him, I didn't have any idea of what an avadhut was. Through years of serving him and seeing the results of interactions with him I got to see good results and bad results. Based on observation and experimentation, I came up with my own ideas of how an avadhut operates and how to interact with them. Much of what I figured out seems like common sense, but I saw over and over

---

[1] An enlightened being in the highest stage, is beyond the five elements, has gone beyond body consciousness and because of that, operates outside the conventions of "normal" behavior; has the ability to command on the creation.

[2] (? – 1918) Great avadhut saint and sadguru.

[3] (1897?-1961) Great avadhut saint and sadguru.

1

that people kept making the same mistakes understanding and handling the avadhut energy.

To understand what Swami gave, you must understand how the avadhut energy operates. It does not follow the norms of society. That energy doesn't make sense to our minds, and especially our egos, but there are ways to approach that energy that will help people to succeed. Even now I see that, although students have done advanced spiritual *sadhanas*, they missed some of the basic concepts and are stuck in their spirituality and are struggling in their lives.

Avadhut translates as unconditional love. An avadhut lives and operates in unconditional love and exists to take care of our souls. But there are certain things that energy requires of us in order to do its job. Even though Swami is no longer in his body, the avadhut energy is still working powerfully in the lives of anyone who has a connection to him and this lineage. It is my hope that through sharing what I learned while serving him, spiritual students can learn how to win God's heart and receive whatever they are eligible for in this lifetime.

Sivapriya Godino:

I first met Terry (Sundaram) when I came to the Divine Mother Center in 2016 for the Guru Purnima program. After one of the *pujas*, I stayed to have more time at the fire. Terry stayed as well (now I know that he always does, since his job is to feed the fire with all the coconuts cracked for blessings) and made a joke about how his favorite time at the fire is after everyone leaves!

By Baba's grace I was blessed to be able to make multiple trips to the Center over that next year, and a kinship emerged between us as we would visit after fire pujas. I can remember those first few talks we had were like picking up a conversation with a friend you haven't seen in years. At first, it's a little awkward, but as the energy of the friendship picks up it is like we had never been apart. I had to keep remembering we were picking up a friendship from another lifetime.

One cold November night, I was asked to go over to let him know that the propane in the main house was broken. I thought I would just deliver the message about the broken heater and leave, but he invited me into his trailer, which was toasty warm from the woodstove, and invited me to sit down. Since the benches were filled with fix-it projects, I grabbed a cushion and put it on the floor near the stove at the foot of his chair. Terry started talking about Swami. I honestly cannot remember what we talked about that night; I can only remember the way the energy changed when he started talking. It was *Dwarkamai* energy. With the broken heater forgotten, we both fell into the bliss of his sharings. Although he cried as he shared (and for months, he could not speak of Swami without bringing both of us to tears), I could see that sharing about his life with Swami had a profound effect on his energy.

I found out later that when Terry served Swami, he could not talk to anyone. Everything about his life was secret, to protect Swami's privacy. He had years of built-up energy that he had received from a supernatural soul. He had been holding years of experiences and knowledge that needed to be shared. Sharing is necessary in the *shakti-energy channels*, otherwise our energy gets stuck.

Sometime later, I got a very difficult reflection in my life about my ego coming up. My defensiveness in the face of that reflection only made things worse. I had the insight to reach out to Terry and we ended up talking for a long time about the avadhut energy, how it works and how to handle it, especially when it presents in a more "punching" way. He helped me understand how to look at what had happened at a mechanistic level, and how my responses had made things worse. It was a turning point in my life, and his words gave me the courage to receive that energy into myself in the way that it was intended, as love.

After our conversation, Terry said he realized how little students understand about how an avadhut operates. The avadhut energy does not follow the rules of our culture. We must re-learn almost everything we know to operate successfully in it. In his eleven years of serving Swami, Terry studied that energy and learned how to win in it by trial and error, by carefully observing his own and other students' mistakes and victories. Until he started helping me try to understand it, he did not realize what he had learned.

How can we understand avadhut energy, how it operates, and how to win in it? How can we translate what he learned when Swami was alive to help us all now? Now that Swami is no longer in the body, how does that energy run in our lives? These are some of the questions that we explored, holding up each memory and looking for clues.

Terry shared some of his insights with Mataji, and she could see what a positive effect sharing his stories was having on him. In true Sri Kaleshwar style, hitting multiple targets with one arrow, she asked us to write a book together about Terry's time with Swami. In 2018, on Shivaratri, we cracked a coconut to bless that project to come into the creation.

The words in this book are one hundred percent Terry's. My job has been to listen, to capture the stories either by recording them or by typing as he talked, and perhaps most importantly, by asking the questions that inspired him to share what often was deeply sensitive material. Mataji has guided us each step of the way, and the entire staff at the Divine Mother Center have supported us in this work. It would not exist without this loving teamwork that Swami so wanted from us all.

For me, this book is a living channel to a great saint, Swami Kaleshwar. It is a dynamic imprint of how the master's *sankalpams* transcend time and come alive through each of our lives. This book is an example of *Sai Shakti Healing*[4], and the necessity of sharing the energy we receive. And best of all, it is a page-turning tale of an immortal friendship between saints.

Working on this book has been one of the most precious blessings God has ever given me. Each of the stories are imprinted on my heart, and they continue to transform me. I pray that this book can be a practical guide to you like it has been to me, and that it lifts and inspires your process. May we each win our master's heart and become eligible for all that Swami promised us, to have a personal relationship with the Divine Mother and become vessels of Her love and power in the creation.

And may we each always be blessed to listen to the stories of the lives of saints, and to sit at their feet.

---

[4] An ancient science of soul healing, transmitting pure cosmic energy to a soul through the Five Elements energy channels. When a person's soul is strengthened in this way, suffering and stuck energy from heartbreak and negative experiences are removed.

INTRODUCTION

by Mataji

My first introduction to the concept of avadhut was in the late 70s in New York City when seeking out teachers from different traditions that had come to America at that time. I attended my first *satsang* in a sprawling upper Westside apartment led by a Buddhist Lama.

During the question-and-answer session after meditation, a person asked the Lama to comment on the controversial behavior of a Tibetan Tantric master living in the United States named *Chogyam Trungpa Rinpoche*[5]. Trungpa coined the term 'crazy wisdom' master, a western colloquialism for an avadhut. After some silence, the Lama replied, "How can I, a creature here on the ground, comment on the great eagle flying in the sky?" I had no inkling how prescient this question was to my life.

Shortly after, I went to live in *Swami Muktananda's*[6] *ashram* in upstate New York. On the walls of the meditation hall hung huge images of mostly naked, big-bellied saints! These great beings were avadhuts and Muktananda often told stories of them in his teachings. It was difficult to understand their strange behaviors. *Zipruanna*[7] sat naked on rotten garbage heaps but was luminous and radiant, smelling like fragrant flowers, unsoiled by the filth around him. It was a demonstration of the purity of his state. *Hari Giri Baba*[8], who wore nine coats, no matter how hot, and had rocks in his pockets, which he would use to throw at people shouting, "This is worth 10,000 *rupees!*" That's how he would kick out their karma! *Bhagavan Nityananda*[9], Swami Muktananda's guru, would lay around mostly naked and when someone would come, he would bless them by repeating a *bija mantra* that sounded like a grunt, *Hun*. An avadhut is always

---

[5] (1939-1987) 11th descendent in the line of Trungpa tulkus, recognized as a pre-eminent teacher of Tibetan Buddhism.

[6] (1908-1982) Founder of Siddha Yoga, disciple of Bhagavan Nityananda.

[7] An avadhut saint from the village of Nasirabad, Maharashtra.

[8] An avadhut saint from Vaijapur, Maharashtra.

[9] (1887 – 1961) said to have been born enlightened.

blessing, whatever they are doing, whatever it looks like is always for your highest good.

Twenty years later, I met Sri Kaleshwar. Swami taught about Shirdi Sai Baba, his guru, who was an avadhut that was often misunderstood by the people. Shirdi Sai was the most tenderhearted, loving grandfather but could scream so badly at someone, Swami said, it was like their skin was peeling off! Shirdi Sai confounded everyone around him. When he demanded money from someone, which he often did, they would run to the other side of the street! "Was Baba crazy?" Swami would ask. "Why do avadhuts act this way? What are they really doing? There is deep meaning behind their actions."

An avadhut is an embodiment of unconditional love, so why would they beat someone with a stick? There was an energy mechanism operating. When Shirdi Baba hit a person with a stick, the person was healed. It required a blow from Baba to balance the karma being removed. Avadhuts understand the laws of karma, and how to use the energy to free someone of it. When Shirdi Baba demanded money, he was giving a blessing, whether it was for washing greed, taking karma, or making someone rich. But whatever he took, it was returned tenfold! It was an energy law, an energy mechanism.

An avadhut's behavior is also a filtering device to test a student. Dattatreya[10], the guru of gurus, is the head of our lineage. When the great Parasurama[11] went to Dattatreya for initiation, he found him sitting with a jug of wine and a beautiful woman on his lap! Dattatreya looked drunk. This shocked Parasurama. He thought, 'Is he a drunkard and womanizer?' This was Dattatreya's test to see if Parasurama could see through his appearance and discriminate what was real. Finally, Parasurama recognized that Dattatreya was no ordinary being. This made him eligible to receive initiation into secret teachings of Mother Divine.

An avadhut's actions cannot be understood by the ordinary mind. They exist for the welfare of the world.

---

[10] The primordial guru from which all lineages ultimately arise, the incarnation of Brahma, Vishnu and Shiva in a single form. Dattatreya (also referred to as Datta) is often depicted as having three heads, symbolizing the three aspects of Creation – creation (Generator), maintenance (Operator) and destruction (Destroyer). Sri Kaleshwar calls Shirdi Baba a pure Dattatreya avatar.

[11] Incarnation of Vishnu.

Swami had a personal interest in having us understand what he called avadhut consciousness. He shared with a few of us that he was going to become avadhut at the end of his life. He wasn't planning to stay long and intended to take *mahasamadhi*. He predicted that people would react against his behavior in the end. "How will people feel if they see me hanging out at a five-star hotel with a bunch of dancing girls?"

It was inconceivable that this gentle, *sattvic* 24-year-old, would act that way. He was polite, refined, and sensitive, incredibly so. He said that when he reprimanded someone, it took him two days to recover! Unfortunately, stronger methods are required to wake us up in this *Kali Yuga*! By nature, by his own estimation, he didn't have a punishing nature. It wasn't his style. But he knew the energy would require that to work on egos. This is a reason a master acts in an avadhut way. Swami's mission was to create spiritual masters, which requires the highest purification. He said it took the same energy for a guru to take care of a million devotees as it did to produce one spiritual master. He was working on souls who would be masters in this or a future life. The aim of the *ancient knowledge*[12] was to create spiritual masters to serve and heal the world.

Why is it so important to understand the consciousness of the avadhut? Although avadhuts are extremely rare, there will be more. They are needed to transform the world and seed a new golden age of consciousness. Many divine souls are coming to this planet. Swami said some of his students would become avadhuts. He believed strongly in the students of this knowledge, "My students will do wonders for peace and harmony in the world."

Swami shared his life very openly with those of us around him. He wanted us to use his life as an example of what it's really like to live in avadhut consciousness. It would help us in our own lives. He told us many times over the years to tell the truth about his life. He didn't want us to sugarcoat the realities of any of it. We had a responsibility to share the truth about his life. It will help the world understand.

Swami was a human being and a divine being. Swami shared his human life very openly with those close to him. He didn't like hiding. He wanted us to be soul mates with him, he said soul mates needed to share everything with each

---

[12] Enlightenment channels given by the Divine Mother contained in the palm leaf manuscripts revealed by Sri Kaleshwar.

other. He modeled that. He also said he was going to change the role of the guru in this age, so the guru is a friend. He modeled that too. Historically, avadhuts have remained distant from society because they are so misunderstood. Their lives have been shrouded in mystery. Swami was unique; he was very open.

Through Terry's eyes, we have a rare glimpse into Swami's private life and how an avadhut operates. We also experience the profound connection between the guru and disciple, and the miracle that takes place through that alchemical relationship.

PART ONE:
THE JOURNEY BEGINS

Swami, 1997

Beginnings

Let us bow now before the great saints. Their merciful glances will destroy mountains of karmas (sins) and do away with all the negative defects of our character. Even their casual talk is a teaching and confers imperishable happiness on us. Their minds do not know differences such as, "This is ours and that is yours." Such differentiation never arises in their minds. We can never repay our debt to them in this life or in many future lives.
-Sri Sai Satcharitra

I met Swami in Malibu in August of 1997. My first impression on meeting him was that he was small. He was like a little kid! But I knew enough to know that his physical age and stature didn't matter, so that wasn't as important to me as what he was teaching, the *Brahma Kundalini Nadi* healing system.

My leg had been badly broken. I had an external bar on the outside of my leg and was on crutches. My leg was shattered; it wasn't a simple break. It didn't feel horrible, but it was bad, and was scary to look at since a metal rod was drilled into my leg from the outside. Gaya, the mother of my friend, Ramakrishna, told me, "You could use a healing. There is a young Indian saint coming and he is really good."

I wasn't interested in anything Indian anymore. I had already had an Indian guru and felt I had gone as far as I could with that experience. But for some reason, I went to Malibu anyway to meet Swami and stayed at Gaya and Ramakrishna's house. Gaya kept telling me to ask Swami for a healing. I thought it seemed obvious that I needed healing, with a big thing hanging off my leg and crutches! But she told me that the way it works is you have to ask, you can't just assume that he will give you a healing.

I positioned myself in a place where Swami had to walk by. He had to walk right in front of me, so I knew this was my chance. As he walked by, I asked him for a healing. He didn't say anything. He clearly heard me, he clearly saw me, but he just walked right by. Some hours later we were meditating in a big yurt. Swami was spinning his arm from the shoulder and *vibhuti* was shooting out of his sleeve. It was like a hose! A huge amount of vibhuti covered the entire room. Swami was spinning his arm and covered a man with it who had cancer. The smell in the room was intoxicating. He went around the yurt and when he came to me, the first thing I thought was that he had thrown hot water on me, and I jumped!

Afterward, he called everyone to a room in a different building. I walked down with my crutches and sat in the back. I had black clothes on, and you could see that the left side of my body was covered in vibhuti, but not the right. It was my left leg that had been broken. A simple fracture is not a big deal, but shattering bone is much more serious. At the time, I was about halfway through the healing process. Within weeks I was able to start weight bearing, and most importantly, I had no complications. It took ten months to finish healing, but I had no problems. Years later Swami commented on our first meeting, that I came with my sticks (crutches)! He remembered that.

That day, after the healing he gave us *mantras*, spelled them, and wanted us to write them down. It was a shock to come to a spiritual teacher and the first thing he said was get your pen and paper out and start writing mantras down. He went around looking at everyone's papers. I was terrified he would come over and I would get kicked out for being such a terrible student.

Swami's accent was so heavy at the time I was thinking, 'I have no idea what he is talking about! It makes no sense!' The parts that I did understand I wrote down, but mostly I was copying off the people around me. I really could not understand what he was saying. Finally, he did come over and corrected only one small thing out of all the things I had wrong. I knew deep inside I couldn't hide anything from him. Even though I couldn't understand him, there was something about him that was just so appealing.

Then he gave us a short mantra that we were going to meditate with all night! It was just a few words. I wrote it on a piece of paper and had to keep taking it out of my pocket; I couldn't remember it because I would immediately go into a trance. I had never experienced that. I had been meditating since my early 20's. I thought I went to sleep.

Swami gave healings and talked to people as he walked around the yurt. He got to the person next to me and I came out of trance. I was a little shocked and worried that he would know that I had fallen asleep. At the end of the meditation, he called on a guy and asked him what his experience was. He said he started doing the mantra, which was hard, but as soon as he started to get it, he went into a trance. He described my experience exactly! Swami told him, "You had that experience because of our deep soul connection."

That was the beginning of seeing that Swami knew what I was experiencing. I didn't recognize it, but he did. He knew he couldn't ask me because I would have said I went to sleep. But the truth was, I didn't, and the energy was so different than anything I had ever experienced. It was impressive. For me that was it.

After the program, Ramakrishna invited me to come to a fire puja so we could hang out with Swami. I asked if he had invited us. Ramakrishna was quite casual; he said it would be fine if I came. I had a little feeling that it might not be, but I went. When we got to where the event was, Ramakrishna talked with Swami, but I stayed a little distant. After a while, Ramakrishna came over and told me I needed to go. I just said no problem. I had no attachment to being around. I completely understood.

The next weekend, I drove to Mill Valley to do the *Shakti Patanjali* workshop. Swami gave us an option in the process to choose a divine soul to connect to: Baba, Swami, or Jesus. My mother was a Sunday school teacher, so I was raised Christian, more or less against my will. So, I would not have chosen Jesus. My feeling was to choose Swami because I felt so much closer to him than anyone. Even then I felt he knew me so well; he was so familiar to me. He came up to me during the process and before I could say anything, he said, "Jesus." I was shocked.

This has consistently been my experience with Swami. So often his behavior was not how I thought a guru or a master would behave. He was different, and different in a beautiful way. Over the years, I would come to see how many ideas and concepts I was carrying about what a master is, and about what it meant to be with a master. He would challenge all of it.

Fire Puja, Los Angeles, 1997

Shakti Patanjali, Mill Valley, CA, 1997

Power Journey to India

The following February, I went to India for a couple of weeks on a power journey. I had never been to India, but I was so surprised that when I stepped off the plane it felt like home. We drove around in a bus and went to many sacred places, samadhis, and temples. We travelled with Swami to Sri Sailam. Sri Sailam is a temple town inside a tiger preserve; the road is closed at night. We were in the bus and Swami was in his personal vehicle. We stopped at a little roadside *dhaba* for tea and snacks. It was close to closing time. People got off the bus and rushed in before it closed. Then Swami got out and stood next to the car. I walked over to say hello. Swami saw me coming and was friendly. I wouldn't have continued my approach if he seemed disinterested. He asked me if I was enjoying the drive. "Do you want to drive?" he said.

Then he motioned to the car door inviting me to drive! Immediately my reaction was no way, I don't want to drive. I had driven big equipment and motorcycles throughout my life and loved driving, but driving with the steering wheel on the right on Indian roads didn't tempt me in the least. Any sane person who has driven on Indian roads would feel the same. Swami was laughing and got a kick from my reaction. His driver, Anthony, was enjoying it too. After our funny interaction, Swami walked away. Then Anthony looked at me and ordered me to get back on the bus. No one else was on the bus! I sat alone on the bus. That was my first interaction with Anthony, Swami's most senior driver who had been with him the longest.

I would come to see that this was natural for Swami, he would often play and tease his students, making them laugh and sharing joyful moments with them.

When we were in America, Swami spoke about the gorgeous ashram[13] he had and about how many people came to visit, thousands of Indians on New Moons and Full Moons. Then I got there, and it was a tiny little building surrounded by dirt and brambles! One thing I observed with Swami is, sometimes when he spoke, he wasn't referring to the current time, he was talking about the future. He was talking about what the ashram *would* become.

---

[13] Siva Sai Mandir, Penukonda, Andhra Pradesh, India.

16

And it did. In a really short time, only a few years. I was there when he started building the first apartment building. He had seen the vision of how it would be. He knew where it was going. It showed me how Swami's perspective on time was so much more than mine.

The hut was the first building of the ashram. It was round with a thatched roof and open to the air and it was where the Indian staff ate. An Indian couple cooked in a huge pot over an open fire. Right next to the hut was Swami's swing, which hung on a huge tamarind tree. Next to that, was a huge statue of *Hanuman*.

Witnessing the Miracle Birth of Atma Lingams

Until Swami, I had a strong aversion to India. My experience was that everyone who went got really sick. But I was lured by going on a power journey with Swami. He was going to birth an *Atma lingam* but that wasn't why I went, although that was part of how the trip was billed. Ramakrishna's mother, Gaya, organized the trip. Her flyer said if you witnessed the birth of an Atma Lingam you wouldn't have to be reborn, along with other incredible claims.

When our group got to the ashram, they drove the bus through the fort entrance. You have to zig-zag and move the electrical wires and jockey the bus to get it through. It was a big deal. The ashram was just a little building with dirt around it and a gazillion weeds and thorn bushes. All the women used the one bathroom in the *Mandir*[14] and the men used the stock tank where you could take a bath in your underwear. You had to stand outside, visible from the Baba Temple. Our whole group of 25 stayed in the Baba Temple. We took the Indian mattresses off the bus and put them on the floor where everyone slept.

Swami was going to birth two lingams, Shiva and Shakti. He gave birth to the Shiva lingam first in the Baba Temple. With the Shiva lingam, there is no blood and it is not as painful, but I wouldn't say it was easy. Ramakrishna was the official catcher; he had a towel in his hand. Swami would drink a lot of water then would hunch over, with Ramakrishna squatting in front of him. He had played baseball, so he was good at catching. If the Atma lingam falls on the

---

[14] Main building in Penukonda ashram, which houses the Baba Temple.

ground it gets absorbed by the earth, it's gone. So, Ramakrishna was chasing Swami all around with his towel. Somebody was trying to film it so, of course, she was in the way with her giant camera so nobody else could see! Part of the instruction was to watch the lingam being birthed with your own eyes.

We were all supposed to be meditating. Swami was in front of Baba, and because it was so painful, he kept moving around which enabled us to see what was happening. The energy was really heavy. I think half the people didn't see it because they were in a trance and nodding off. Fortunately, Gaya said something right about the time it was to be birthed. I went over and saw Swami birth the Atma lingam, spitting it out like an olive! It wasn't a slow process; it flew right out of his mouth. Even with the lights turned down, I did see it clearly.

Then we all took the same bus to Sri Sailam for the birth of the Shakti lingam. He did this in front of the pilgrim bungalows where we were staying. He gave it to Mataji. I witnessed that one too.

Guru Raghavendra's Samadhi

On the bus trip, we visited the *jiva samadhi* of *Guru Raghavendra*[15]. This was my first experience of a jiva samadhi. You could feel the waves of energy emanating from the place as soon as we got off the bus! I was struck by it. I had never been anywhere where it was so strong. I learned a jiva samadhi can emanate energy for hundreds or thousands of years. Raghavendra's samadhi was 400 years old.

The energy was so strong, I could feel it as soon as we got off the bus. Every step up the hill leading to it, it got stronger. I didn't know much about samadhis. I had gone to the Vatican in 1978 and thought that place was dead. I didn't feel any big energy there. I didn't know anything about the mechanisms of saints' samadhis at the time, but I felt the energy, it was so strong. It really made an impression on me.

---

[15] (1595-1671)

Many Lifetimes Together

We don't want, you don't want, a normal, simple life. To know who you are, to know the greatness of supernatural spirituality, the secrecy hidden in nature, the secrecy of consciousness, and the secrecy of avadhut consciousness. What is birth? What is death? Where is the beginning? Where is the ending? You need to learn that.

-Sri Kaleshwar

Near the end of the power journey trip, we were staying in Hyderabad at the Amruta Castle, a Best Western-style hotel styled after the Knights of the Round Table! It was designed to look like a castle, even had armor in the lobby. Swami asked if I wanted a personal interview. I was leaving the power journey to finish physical therapy to make sure my leg was healed. I didn't really have any questions, but I did want to spend time with him.

I went in his room; I think that he stayed in the Sri Lancelot suite. I was escorted in, and Swami asked me if I had any questions. I did ask something, but it wasn't a big deal. I was alone with him for the first time. He told me then that we had had many lifetimes together, and our connection was close. He said to just call on him anytime and he would be there.

At the end, he asked me to stand up so he could do a healing on me. He had a long-stemmed rose and gave me *shaktipat* on my third eye. Then he spun his hand, manifested a ring, and put it on my little finger. It fit. I still have that ring; it's a silver ring with a white stone. He gave me a lot of rings over the years. I had rings for all my fingers!

I didn't have much interest in going to India until I met Swami. Most of my friends who had gone to India came back with dysentery. But after the trip, I knew I wanted to spend more time there.

Sri Sailam, 1998

Mantralayam, 1998

Swami and Terry meditating, Mantralayam, 1998

Sri Sailam, 1998

Manifesting kum kum, Sri Sailam, 1998

Manifesting kum kum, Sri Sailam, 1998

Teaching the Sri Chakra, Shirdi, 1998

Power journey bus arrives, 1998

Shiva Cave, 1998

Ganesh Temple, 1998

Mandir Entrance, 1998

Move to India

Soon after returning home from the power journey, I wanted to go back to India. In the spring of the next year, I was at a *Toltec* event with Ramakrishna and asked him about going back. He encouraged me to go. I told him I thought I needed permission. He said no problem, he could call Swami. Ramakrishna dialed Swami in India and woke him up and asked if I could come to India. Swami said yes, he remembered me, and said I could come. Ramakrishna looked at me and asked when I could go. That was April, I said maybe by June. That is how I got permission to go back.

I went back to India to stay. I quit my job and stored my stuff, and my feeling was I had basically left America. Swami had told us that we can become like him, that we were all healers and that it was possible for us to do what he did. He said the only difference between us and him was knowledge. He knew certain things that we didn't yet know, and experiencing firsthand my own healing was such an enticement.

When I first arrived in India, there were only a few Westerners in the ashram, mostly Indian staff. I was clear that I wanted something and had a reason to be there, so I really didn't want to waste my time. One main thing was *japa*. By then, the mantras started to make sense since I had repeated them a lot while my leg was healing, and I wasn't working. I did a lot of japa before I ever got to India. I did the *Brahma Kundalini Nadi* mantras plus the Five Elements mantras.

I didn't expect Swami to teach me personally when I was there. I thought he would have students that I would learn from. I thought I didn't need to take his time. He was busy and had all these people coming. When I arrived, he told me to do the Five Elements mantras. So, for many months, I sat under a tree and did japa all day.

"I am staying until you throw me out!"

My girlfriend, Michelle, had never met Swami, but had heard me talk about him. She knew I wanted to go to India and stay, I thought maybe for a couple of years. Little did I know it would be thirteen years! Michelle decided that she wanted to go with me then. So, we flew together. Michelle was only going to stay for a short time then head back to America.

In Bangalore, we got a driver and car to take us to the ashram. At that time, Swami wasn't that well known. We drove right up to the front of the Mandir. Swami was by the dhuni and walked over to greet us. He asked me, "How long are you staying?"

"I am staying until you throw me out!" Swami seemed to really like that. I had saved up enough money that I could stay in India for an indefinite amount of time. Other people would come but only had enough money to stay for a finite amount of time. For me, it was different because I had enough money to stay as long as I needed. He liked that. I didn't realize how much, but later he commented on that.

It didn't get any reaction from him in the moment. I found out later he had been very happy with that answer because I could stay as long as I needed.

Another student who came around the same time had worked for a tech company. She had made lots of money, cashed out, then went to India. She had money but had left a complex lifestyle behind, so still had a lot of expenses. She knew she could only stay for a limited time, maybe six months or a year. Swami didn't like that it was limited. She wanted to receive; she wanted to do processes, but there was a limitation. Also, there was the financial thing; she always had to worry about it. She wasn't free.

Later he made an example of me, that I came with no fixed return, and came with enough money to support myself. I had worked hard for years and lived frugally to save money. I had saved enough to live off the interest and stay indefinitely.

Seeing the Divine in Him

I didn't see Swami so much as a friend. I saw his humanness, but I didn't want to concentrate on that. I wanted to see and hold the divine above the human. I always related to the divine part of him. A part of that attitude could be that I had had a guru earlier.

When I was 19, I was initiated into my first guru's lineage in Tucson. Everyone said that if you have a connection in your heart, you can experience it anywhere even if you are not around him. I was familiar with that concept and experienced that feeling of being close to him even without being physically close. I went to work for my guru's company in Florida. You had to follow certain protocols. For example, if he talked to you then you could talk to him. You could never approach him directly; you could never initiate a conversation. You had to wait for him to initiate. He was particular about who he interacted with. He would interact with certain people more.

When the guru would come, we were told not to stare at him. We should talk only if he talked to us but otherwise should not approach him. He would come and walk around the factory floor. If he came, we would have to stop working since the work was noisy. He had a garage for his cars that was separate from the manufacturing area. Sometimes I would be invited to the garage to do special projects or give some machine or welding help. If the guru came, the first thing they did was kick everybody out. So they would run me off. I knew I had an internal connection to him, so I was comfortable with that.

That training carried over to my life with Swami. In India, there are lots of rules to follow to show respect to a guru. You never stand taller than him, you never cross his shadow, you never approach him without permission. Awareness of these things helped with my relationship with him. I didn't think about it then, but I realize now that a part of winning his heart was my previous training. I tended not to be so casual in my interactions with him. He never proclaimed he was a guru or that anyone needed to bow to him, but I felt that he needed to be respected and I didn't want my interactions with him to be casual.

I saw it as a big part of being around him, to operate from a place of respect for him. I always approached him with a respectful nature. Some students had more of a friendly relationship with him, but my attitude was always to be aware that he was an avadhut. You need to respect him no matter what is happening. It could be friendly and low-key, but that could change in a minute, to all business. It was important not to lose sight of that and be able to change as quickly as he did. For me, it was better not to fall into the friendly category and then have to jump back. It was better to not be too friendly. I didn't want to compromise my relationship with him.

He Knows Me

After some time at the ashram, I was asked to help with Swami's phone. Swami had just gotten a new phone from Singapore. It was a long-range cordless phone. One of the Indian staff had hooked it up but couldn't get it to work. Swami wanted it fixed. Somebody asked me to look at it since I was a mechanic. It was the first time I went into Swami's living area. The phone had a little black power box that had a switch for different voltages. It only took me a few minutes to figure out the wrong power setting had been used and it had blown out the power cord. Swami came into the room and was checking on me. I had talked to him before, but I felt a little odd being in his living area. I told him I believed the only problem was the power supply, and if they replaced it the phone would work. Of course, Swami was hoping that I could have fixed it right away, but replacing the power supply was easier than replacing the whole phone, so he was happy about that. After that, I began to have more interactions with Swami.

Soon after, I started my meditations out under the tree in the Northwest of the ashram.

At the time, Swami started doing *Vaastu* improvements and was knocking walls down and putting new ones up. He would knock down a wall then put another one up a couple of feet away! Every day he would come out of the Mandir and would walk across the courtyard in front of me, and often would look at me. Mostly I would have my eyes closed because I was meditating, but I could feel him pull on me. I would open my eyes and then he would always wave, and then away he would go.

He would also show me he knew what inner experiences I was having. He would give teachings during the program and say something like, if you do this mantra, you can have these kinds of experiences. Often, as he would describe the experience, he would look directly at me. Many of the things he described had happened to me. I had no idea why I had those experiences. I had no explanation. Then in a public program he would indirectly, or very directly, describe it then look at me. It was like he was checking to see if I knew that I had it. 'Were you aware of what was going on?' He was showing me that he knew exactly what was going on in me. He wouldn't ask me or talk directly to me about it. He would let on indirectly. It was clear that he knew what experiences I was having. Talking to me was not necessary.

I began to feel when Swami was thinking of me. One time, we were doing a process repeating a new mantra he had given. Most of the people were much quicker learning new mantras than me. I was a little slow. It took me longer, especially if they had new words. Swami called everyone into the Baba Temple to ask people how many *malas* of japa repetition they had done. Some people had done a lot. I had done a fair amount. I was applying myself, but other people were much faster than me. Swami went around the room asking people to repeat the mantra. He was appearing to get angry. He would ask, "How many malas did you do?" Then he would ask them to say the mantra. He was upset. He said, "You're all doing these mantras but can't pronounce it?" The truth is, if Swami put his attention on you, you really couldn't remember anything. Even if you knew it perfectly, it would fly out of your head. For me, it was always scary when he did that. The worst thing was, I could feel it in my solar plexus when he was thinking about me or was going to call on me. It was not pleasant.

I got that feeling in my solar plexus, and sure enough, Swami asked, "Terry, how many malas have you done?" I told him. Then he told me to say the mantra. It was always terrible for me to have to speak in public. Of course, I couldn't think of anything. I couldn't even remember *Om*. My mind was completely blank. But there was a German woman sitting off to my right. I didn't know her. When Swami called on me, she had her head down with her hand in front of her mouth, resting her forehead on her knee. She just said the mantra word by word. She started with *Om*, and then said it slowly word by word. She would say a word then I would repeat it. I said the whole mantra perfectly. The look on Swami's face was priceless! He was shocked. It was one of the few times I saw that kind of surprise on his face. I got a real kick out of that.

Satsang: Swami Heals My Heartbreak

Ashram, Penukonda, 1999

SWAMI: Ok, one more person (to share their heartbreak experience). It's good to hear because I can pull out a lot of points. Ah, why can't I ask Terry?

Terry: What example would you like? A new one or an old one?

SWAMI: Well, a new one.

Terry: How about two nights ago?

SWAMI: Jonathan said he stagnated for about two and half years. He came here, but he didn't know why he wanted to be here. Then he ran away. Big confusion. Finally, now he's here. I'm going to talk about a few people's personal lives too, the heart feelings, what type of illusions they're carrying, what type of energy they're carrying, how to break it very easily.

Jonathan: Oh, I should add one thing, Swami. This will make your picture more complete. While that unhappiness was going on, while that confusion was there, I was still doing amazing healings and miraculous things were happening out in the world. That was still happening. It was strange.

SWAMI: Good, beautiful. Your life is so beautiful, no need to worry. Terry?

Terry: There have been some things that Swami has asked me to do.

SWAMI: What?

Terry: You would ask me to do something.

SWAMI: Like what?

Terry: Saying things in public. I'm not used to speaking in public. So, you would ask me to do that.

SWAMI: Hey, you're going to become as a teacher, isn't it?

Terry: Yes.

SWAMI: You have to talk in public.

Terry: Yes. I have before and I haven't had any trouble. Some but not a lot. But here, much more.

SWAMI: Why?

Terry: Partially, my insecurity.

SWAMI: What?

Terry: I'm insecure about speaking in public, so it comes up. So naturally you will ask me to do that.

SWAMI: It means I'm cruel there?

Terry: No, it means I need to practice and you're going to push me to practice.

SWAMI: Ah hun. What are your feelings at the time?

Terry: Ah, it could be that you're picking on me. I could feel that you're picking on me. That you're not understanding that I'm having trouble speaking in public. It's unfair.

SWAMI: It's unfair? To you or to me?

Terry: Well, obviously not to you. To me. Then I could… get upset.

SWAMI: How much did you get upset? I'm so sorry.

Terry: Quite a lot.

SWAMI: Quite a lot? No way. I'm a big rakshasa on my duty. Once I want to train you… I really care about your feelings, everybody's feelings, Part A. Part B, same time, I'm also very sensitive. Part C, I'm a big rakshasa; I totally ignore everything and handle it with a [knife's] edge, making it, fixing it. Otherwise, if I let you go on like that five years, seven years, ten, you won't get it. You know what I'm saying? No way, you can get it. It's not a punishment. I hate to give punishment. That's not my nature at all. To create a little pain there, just a little bit, not staying a long time. You have to fix it yourself. You have to heal it yourself, then you can walk out. If you're not walking out, then I'm there to help you. It's not a good example. One more, tell your personal life, where you were really heartbroken.

Terry: With a relationship? That's where I mainly got heartbroken.

SWAMI: Go ahead, talk. I know how much you're very self-sensitive. It's not fair for me now to even talk to you about that, but it's necessary. Everybody has to learn the illusions, the blocks, how to wash them out. I'm so sorry I have to pick you.

Terry: That's fine. So probably the worst one was my first serious relationship. I started to see that it wasn't going so well but I chose to ignore that. So, the relationship continued to go. Then I was very pulled to the spiritual path. I was on the spiritual path and she wasn't, so I started to see that we were going in different directions although again I chose to ignore that. The final thing was finding a letter that she had written. A love letter that she had written to someone else.

SWAMI: You read that?

Terry: Yes, she left it out on top of her dresser, in an obvious place. I was in the room and there it was. I was devastated.

SWAMI: How did you survive that? How much time it took you?

Terry: That took years.

SWAMI: Years?

Terry: Yes.

SWAMI: How much?

Terry: Two or three.

SWAMI: That same energy you can heal within two to three hours! I can give the medicine, spiritual medicine right now. Does anybody have such type of feelings in your life?

He Knows What I Am Thinking

There were only four Westerners at the ashram when I arrived. We were staying above the Mandir where the Jesus Temple is now. It was the summer solstice, so we decided to do a little meditation. Swami was busy with the Indian devotees. This was when thousands would come on the Full Moon and New Moon to receive his blessings.

We sat back-to-back forming a cross. I don't think we went ten minutes when Swami came up the stairs and asked what we were doing. He wasn't upset, some energy was running, and he was coming to see. We told him we were just doing a little meditation. Swami had one of the Indian staff get a chair, then sat down and started talking. What he was saying didn't appear to have anything to do with what we were doing. It was the energy we were generating that drew him making it possible for us to receive knowledge.

He talked about some very interesting things I would not have expected a saint to discuss. At the same time, he told us that he wanted a massage. Although there was a massage therapist among us who even taught massage, he looked at me. Swami wanted me! He wanted me to give him a shoulder massage. I was so surprised that he would choose me over a professional.

I would find out later that anytime you touch Swami, he would feel everything. If you have direct physical contact with him, he can see everything in your mind.

It didn't take too long before he asked for me to massage him again. This time it was his legs. He was in a chair. I was sitting on the ground in front of him and started with his feet going up to his calves. I knew enough to massage towards the heart. Swami was so small then. He had already told me, "You have to give a massage with heavy pressure." I had been doing construction work, so I was strong. I'm going up his calf and felt like I could easily squeeze it and break it off. My massage technique was non-existent. I was making the best of it but didn't really know anything about massage. In the middle of that, I was thinking, 'He is just bones, he is so small; he is just going to break off! I could just squash him.'

Right then, he says, "You know you are not going to break your Swami!" He confirmed he knew what I was thinking. I realized then I had to be careful about what I concentrated on when I was around him.

A few days later, he had me massage his shoulders. I noticed he had some gray hair and was surprised since he was so young, and his hair always looked so nice. I could see some gray at the roots at the back of his neck. The next day the hair dye came out! Of course, I hoped I hadn't offended him by noticing his gray hairs. I couldn't have cared less if Swami had gray hair, or if he dyed his hair.

I can say that Swami was showing me that he had a foot in both worlds. I have seen Swami do huge miracles, then be the guy that dyed his hair to make it look good. It wasn't a big deal to me. I was a little surprised at first. But then it was natural. He was human.

On *Guru Purnima*, we had to touch our *power spots* in the Dwarkamai while repeating our *personal mantras*. Swami was inside, sitting on his bed. I was distracted by him and so when I pranamed to touch my power spot, I forgot to say my personal mantra. I said it up until I had seen him, then I just forgot at the last minute. He knew it. "You didn't say your personal mantra." This was in the Dwarkamai, his place of power. He had an angel reading my mind.

One time Swami asked me to massage him at his northeast bed. He said to repeat the *Nine Arrows* mantras. I started saying them silently, then after a little while he complained that I was making mistakes! Then he said everyone in the ashram had to review the *Nine Arrows* the next day. We all had to go to the Mandir to have our pronunciation checked. I had the accent on a bunch of the syllables wrong. For me, that was spectacularly good, just tiny mistakes. Some other students really had them wrong.

He had told us we had to be able to repeat the *Nine Arrows* perfectly. Originally, he said to use only one arrow on a problem, then if that didn't work, use another. Later he changed that. We could repeat all of them at a time. He wanted us to be able to start in any order and go around. We should be able to say them backward! We had to know them that well. He could tell when I massaged him that I did not know them up to his standards, even without me saying them out loud!

There were multiple times like that when he would say something simple, letting me know he knew exactly where I was emotionally and mentally. That continued throughout my time with him.

I knew that Swami could know anything about me. I knew he just could send an angel to check on me. He could know exactly what I had said word for word in a conversation he wasn't a part of. There were a lot of things I didn't know how he knew, but he knew. Even things I was just thinking or feeling. I saw that so many times; he knew things about me no one could know. If he asked me a question, I would always answer straightly. I knew he could always find out if I was telling the truth anyway. Sometimes he knew, and my assumption was he could always find out, so it was better just to tell the truth. I didn't always tell the whole truth, but whatever I did say was true! I figured if he didn't ask more questions, I wasn't volunteering to stick my own foot in my mouth.

My personal experience was he knew exactly where I was and where he was going to take me. He knew where my value lay, where my strengths lay, what my capacity was. It took me years to figure that out. But I felt clearly he knew right away where I would end up, what my capacity was.

One time I was standing on the edge of the verandah in the Jesus Temple, having some very dark thoughts. I was looking off and thinking, 'If I just dive off and hit the slates below that would do it.' What triggered it, I don't even remember now. 'Ok, I gave up my whole life. I am here meditating every day, is this it? Is this all that there is?? I don't think this is enough.'

This was one of those times that Swami just snuck up on me. He showed up at the right time. I was looking over the edge. When he came, I was surprised, and a little bit guilty because of what I was thinking.

As a complete distraction, he asked me, "What's in the bag?' I didn't expect that. I expected he would be upset, or reprimand me for thinking crazy thoughts. Instead, he went in a completely different direction and asked, "What's in the bag?" I said I had a little Singapore Airlines bag as my toiletry bag.

He talked to me a little bit but didn't ask me about what I was thinking or doing. His energy was very light and friendly; he was almost smiling. I felt he knew exactly what I was up to, and the energy had brought him there. But he didn't acknowledge that. Within a few minutes, my energy had completely changed. He had completely washed those thoughts out.

Later, Swami was talking to a group and suddenly in the middle of the talk, he said it was normal to have dark thoughts and to think of suicide. It's a natural part of being spiritual. It will come up.[16] Then he turned to me and asked how often I thought about suicide. I said, "Today, or in general?" Everyone laughed, but then I said, "Often." He was telling me that he knew.

Another student came up to me later and acknowledged that he has had those thoughts and was surprised I would say them in public. My response was, "Swami asked me in particular because he knew, and it's the truth." He seemed to appreciate what I had said. He appreciated my honesty.

---

[16] Spiritual seekers of every tradition face the 'Dark Night of the Soul'. Sri Kaleshwar says to just observe these states of mind, which are fleeting. Suicide is never a solution for the problems we face while embodied. Those who commit suicide become stuck in the negative spirit realm, where their suffering continues until they are released.

Terry eating in the hut

Swami in his swing sitting with his parents

In His Swing

My friends *Mataji*,[17] Philip, and I asked Swami's permission to eat in the hut. We thought the food there was much better than the food they were bringing from the dhaba in town. Often, we would be in the hut eating and Swami would come to the swing and sit down. Because Mataji and Philip had been with Swami Muktananda, they understood, like I did, that we should not pull on him. He would sit in his swing and if we ignored him, and didn't energetically pull on him, he would often invite us to sit with him, and share his food. If we didn't have a full plate of food, he would share some of his with us. You get the master's attention by not chasing or feeling entitled to it.

Swami would often sit in his swing. At that time, the students had to walk right by him to get to the student housing. I would just try and go by without pulling on him. If he said hello, it was fine; if he didn't, it was fine. It was always nice if he said something, but it was fine if he didn't. I would just go to the hut and eat.

When Swami was in his swing meeting with someone, I would turn around and go back. Swami noticed that, and told me not to turn around, that I should go eat. But still, I recognized it was rare for people to get private time with him, and I wanted them to be able to speak freely with him and have privacy, not have someone listening in.

But Swami said I should eat, whoever was there. Each day I would carry my plate and water bottle to eat in the hut. I had a favorite plate that was a little different than most of the others; it was a little thicker and didn't have a rolled edge. One day I went to the hut with a different plate with a rolled edge. Swami noticed and commented on it. He noticed that I had changed plates! They looked very similar but for him to notice that subtle difference surprised me. He asked me why I had a different plate that day. The reason was, there had been no water that morning and I had used the plate for breakfast and couldn't wash it. Unbeknownst to me, the plumbers were in the hut eating. As soon as I told him that, Swami asked the plumbers why the water wasn't running. They immediately got up and left to fix it. All because Swami noticed I had a different

---

[17] Aka Monika Penukonda.

plate. He noticed the smallest details, everything you did. How did he notice, why did he notice, I can't say, but he did.

By the Fire

Swami gave me a process to sit at his *dhuni* and be with the fire. I was charging the fire element. Swami told me I should face north when I meditated. So I sat facing north which is where he would sit.

Anthony would bring out Swami's cot, putting it down with a clang letting me know Swami was on his way. Then Swami would come out and we would sit there together.

One night, while we were both looking at the flames, I noticed the flames, the different colors. I didn't say anything to him. Then Swami commented on how beautiful the fire was and told me that he could write a whole book or Bible just on the fire, just on that one element. I told him I would like to read that book!

Harrison Ford

I was sitting at Swami's dhuni with a group of Westerners. He asked if everyone had an Indian name, I raised my hand to indicate I didn't. That was the time that Swami had watched *Air Force One* with Harrison Ford, so he gave me the name Harrison Ford! He was laughing when he gave it to me.

The next time, I was sitting in the Jesus Temple with all the other students in the ashram. He asked if there was anyone who didn't have an Indian name, so I raised my hand again. This time he said, "Sundaram." I wasn't familiar with the name. I had never heard it until he gave it to me, so I researched it in a bunch of different books. Sundaram is also a name for Shiva. It was Shiva's name before he married Parvati. Shiva had invited a bunch of *rakshasas* to the wedding, and the bride's father was not happy. It turns out that Swami never used that name, he always called me Terry. Once in a great while, he may have said it, but it was extremely rare.

Swami called me 'darling' for a while. It was odd to have another man call me darling. It turns out Swami had just learned that word and was told it was a term of endearment, so he was trying it out. It was odd but sweet. Swami would often use words in funny ways. He could have known it was an unusual way to use that word and did it on purpose to see how I would react, or he could have not known that it was unusual for a man to call another man darling! He did it for a little while and then stopped.

Years later he would call me 'Godfather,' which was the nickname he used the longest. For me, it was a term of endearment. I was older than he was and was trying to take care of him. I felt it was his appreciation of me. He didn't give a lot of that.

At the end of his life, Swami was calling me 'Boss,' which I always thought was very ironic since he was clearly the boss. He called other people Boss. Boss kind of bothered me. It was a little uncomfortable since I never really felt that way.

Sometimes I would be called Terence. Swami heard it and said, "Why is she calling you that?" I told him that Terry is a nickname for someone whose real name was Terence, for a man, or Teresa for a woman. "But my name is not Terence; it's just Terry." For some reason, Swami got the biggest kick out of this.

"Your name is a nickname? You are a nickname!" I told him it could end with a 'y' or an 'i'. You can't tell if it is a man or a woman. He got an even bigger kick out of that. I told him there was a famous singer who is a woman with the exact same name, Terry Clark. And, even more confusing, there's another musician who is Clark Terry, same name backward! His first name is Clark and his last name is Terry. Swami got an even bigger kick out of that. He found it all so funny. Especially that Terry is a nickname, not a real name! I think it was one of those things he was digging to see if I felt bad about it, he would have had a field day with it to suss it out. The truth is, I didn't name myself! My father wanted Terry; he didn't want Terence. He picked Terry; he liked it.

Being Taught Indirectly

Before the Jesus Temple was built, Swami lived in his apartment on the ground floor of the Mandir. I was staying in the room directly above his, which later became his bedroom. I used to meditate a lot up there. He was a little particular about who would stay there because people would stomp hard enough to bother him.

At that time, Swami hadn't started talking about having Mother Divine darshan, but he had given some people an experience of seeing angels. I wasn't there when they did that, but I heard about it. When I was staying in that room, sometimes I would wake up at night and hear angels singing. It was like a choir, the beautiful high-pitched voices of a chorus singing. The thing about it was if you tried to really listen it would go away. You could only hear it if you didn't really try. By ignoring it, it would get louder. I could never make out the words of what they were singing but I could clearly hear it. I would often wake up and hear it. It went for weeks like that, waking up late at night hearing the angels singing.

One night when I woke up and heard the singing, I was overwhelmed by the smell of perfume. I thought Swami had dropped some perfume on the floor, it was just so strong. Then at a public program, he started talking about how to tell if you are in the presence of an angel. One of the symptoms is an overwhelming fragrance like somebody dropped perfume! He gave the exact example I had thought. Then he looked right at me as if to say, 'Are you listening, do you realize what experience you had?'

Swami didn't teach me things directly. It was common that I would have an experience, or notice something unusual, then he would talk about that exact thing in public. He never said anything directly to me, but he knew about the experiences I was having.

Hanging Out

Swami gave the men in the ashram a process to do in the Jesus Temple. We each had to light candles and meditate until the candles burned down. Afterward, we had to go downstairs to do *pradakshina* around the Mandir.

I liked to do it late at night when nobody was there, around ten to midnight. Almost every night when I was doing pradakshina, Swami would come out and talk to me. Mostly he was conversational; it wasn't about the process or anything important. He seemed to just come to hang out and talk.

He was consistent, even though my time varied. It was dark, everything was dark, but he would show up and we would hang out and talk. It was very sweet.

It was very unusual that he would show up every night whenever I was there. He was paying attention to me. When he was talking to me, at first, I would be thinking, 'Well, I need to finish my pradakshinas.' Pretty quickly I realized that he's the one who gave the process and he's the one interrupting it. I would rather spend the time with him; that was the most important thing.

When we talked, it was very casual. It was the one time where we interacted as friends. He was not giving instructions, not commenting on processes. He would do all the talking. I really enjoyed it. After he had come a couple of times, I thought it was exceptional. But then he kept coming...every night! It was dark, he would come out of the Mandir office and wait near the stairs, but I wouldn't necessarily see him. I was absorbed in repeating the mantra and doing pradakshina. When I did see him, I would go sit with him.

After he did that for some time, I had the thought, 'Well, maybe I will see him this time.' Then he quit coming! As soon as I expected he might be there, he didn't come back. Having expectations, even just thinking about it, was enough to kill it with Swami!

Massaging Swami's Feet

I was given a message that Swami wanted me to massage his feet every day. I had to find him and put cream on his feet and massage them. I was shocked. He liked Ponds, but I used some other kind of skin lotion. It went for months. Every day, usually in the afternoon or early evening I would have to find him and ask him if it was a good time. Sometimes he would say yes, or sometimes he would say later. Often, he was talking to people and would just have me sit there and massage his feet. His feet were very dry and cracked because he walked barefoot a lot, and his feet were quite tough. He always liked his toes cracked, so I started doing that too. When I was finished, I would massage the cream that was left into my own hands. His feet didn't seem to get any softer, but my hands did!

One time, Swami called me and wanted to be massaged very firmly. I was quite muscular then so I could squeeze hard, which he seemed to prefer. I was really working at it. I had been there for a long time. He told me I was done, then I left.

Immediately I started to get sick. I had received too much energy! I needed to *decharge* to balance the energy. He had taught decharging techniques and gave specific symptoms when you need to decharge. As soon as I left, I could feel it. Every symptom he said, I had!

The symptoms of needing to decharge, I had all of them; stomach upset, nausea, no appetite, headache, and mental agitation. The biggest one was that my stomach was bothering me.

The first thing I did was quit meditating, because then you are just getting more energy. I used a black stone to decharge, and still wasn't getting better. My stomach was bothering me, which never happened before. I put my feet in a bucket with rose water and decharged. I did three or four techniques, but wasn't getting any better. The next day, the flower guy came, and I bought roses. I put a rose on my navel, the stomachache went away immediately. I had tried decharging with a rose in my hand and with my thumb in the rose, but I hadn't tried putting it on my navel. The symptoms went away immediately when I put the rose on my belly. It took me two days to figure it out.

Swami made some public comment about it later. He asked me what the symptoms were of having too much energy. The question he asked me in public was ambiguous, anyone else who heard the question would have no idea what he was saying. He said something like, energy is energy, it's not good or bad, if you have too much you need to decharge. "Right, Terry?"

I don't know what he had been doing, but his calves and his feet were so strange. The other times I massaged his feet, they were never like that. My impression was that he did that on purpose, he was giving me a lot of energy. Sometimes I thought he was like, yahoo, let's see what happens! Let's blast him and see what he does.

He Wanted Me Around

Swami had called me to the Jesus Temple. He had someone come get me and bring me to him. He was with Babu, the barber. Swami was getting his haircut. Before, they had always run us all off. This time he called me over and had me sit at the top of the stairs. He talked to me but didn't seem to be really interested in anything. So, I just kind of watched him getting his haircut, then when he was done, he sent me away. This was within weeks or months of being in India.

It was strange. If he would have called me over and talked to me, it would have been one thing. He did talk a little, but it was completely superficial fluff. He clearly didn't want to talk, there was some reason he just wanted me around.

Marriage Leelas Begin

The story begins like this. The hottest part of the year in India is around Shivaratri and that year some people had gotten sick, so Swami sent the Westerners back to their countries. I had expected that Swami would have senior students teaching. I didn't have an expectation that he would teach anything. The way he had talked about his ashram, I assumed he had lots of people there. Swami spent his time at his swing or out by the fire. Having no expectation that he would teach, I just started meditating.

But then one day, Swami asked my girlfriend, Michelle, and I when we were going to get married! It was such a shock. It was the last thing I wanted. Even though I was travelling with her, I had no interest in getting married. I had seen marriage as a prison with obligations I could never meet. Michelle had five kids, house payments, car payments, and was living in suburbia! I liked her and lived with her before going to India, but my whole idea of going to India was to purely dedicate my time and life to spiritual pursuits. Swami had said the only difference between him and us was knowledge; he knew certain things that we didn't know yet. I wanted to pursue that. The idea of getting married was completely contrary to everything I wanted. I had enough money saved up to live in a third world country for a long time, but to help finance Michelle, it wouldn't be anything. I tried to understand what the whole idea of marriage meant. To me, it certainly meant financial responsibility; you have to work and provide for your family. That did not go well with my plan of living in India.

Swami then told Michelle if she came back for Guru Purnima in July, we would get married! He didn't ask me. She was super happy. I was super nervous. I didn't really want to do it; I couldn't see any point to it. It didn't make any sense. Why would I get married now? Swami said something to me about when diving in cold water, you just have to practice a little then jump. That wasn't a whole lot of help. But, in the end, I jumped.

It turns out, the first Hindu wedding I saw was my own. I had never seen one, and never thought about having one. It was a big deal; it was on Guru Purnima. Thousands of Indians were there with the Westerners. Nityanandaji came as I was getting dressed and gave me some instructions. Part of it was, you aren't going to have any idea what they're doing, just go along with it. It was true, I had no idea. The priests and Swami got a big kick out of that. Everyone's attention was on me, and I had no idea what was going on. This was on multiple levels.

An interesting incident had happened earlier. Swami had given Michelle a package and told her to meditate with it. Somewhere along the line, she figured out it was a ring. I already had a ring that Swami had given me. Michelle also wanted a ring. Sometime later, Swami told her she could open the box. It was a three-stone diamond ring. She was so happy. For her, it felt like a wedding ring. She put the ring on, but it didn't fit.

I told her that Swami had fixed the size on my ring. When we saw Swami, we could ask him. He was sitting in the place that would eventually become the Dwarkamai. We were walking by when he called us over. We sat with him and had a nice conversation. Then Michelle brought up the ring. He asked to see it, so she handed it to him.

He said, "It's not the right size, huh?" Then he took the ring and put it on my ring finger. "Now it's the perfect size!"

The look on her face! She was shocked but told me later that Swami said the ring was actually for me, that is why it was a perfect size. But I think she really wanted it.

The symbolism of this did not escape me.

Not long after our wedding, Swami was at his swing giving interviews. He was about to leave the ashram to go to *Laytonville*[18] to do a program and everyone in the ashram was leaving to go back to their countries. In our interview, he let Michelle choose how long we were going to be in America. She chose to invite my brother and mother for Thanksgiving in America. This was

---

[18] Now the Divine Mother Center.

September, so I was going to have to stay at her house until November. Swami had told Michelle that when we got married, she could choose how long we would go back to America. I never got a vote in the decision. If he had asked me, I would have gone to America, been there for a week, then come back to India as quickly as possible. Truthfully, I felt like a pawn in the whole thing and wasn't very happy about it.

Swami was sending people off and telling them they needed to go back to their countries and start meditation centers. He gave general instructions but similar for mostly everyone in the group. He was very serious about starting these centers. My intention was to come back as soon as possible. I knew my dharma was in India, not in America. It was clear: I wasn't going to stay there and start a meditation center.

After he got done giving his instructions, he asked a few people what their plans were when they got home. He gets to me and I tell him, "I'm going to ride my motorcycle, drink beer, and smoke cigars." The look on his face! He had a grin that was priceless. Michelle hit me; she was so embarrassed. It was one of those few times I saw him shocked, and I was kind of happy about that.

Michelle went back and forth to America for a year, and I adjusted to being married and to her coming and going. There's more to come about this *leela*. Although it took a while to see what Swami was doing, I did come to understand and appreciate it. It turned out to be as a huge blessing in my life. Most of all, it taught me about the depth of surrender and how that brings you close to the master's heart.

PART TWO:
MIRACLE ENERGY

Swami with bird after Khandana Yoga

Witnessing Khandana Yoga

Shirdi Baba used to do Khandana Yoga, separating his body pieces then again reassembling them. A few people here also did Khandana Yoga. It is not a normal subject of spirituality. It's spirituality beyond spirituality. It is to experience the depth of how the cosmic energy can directly impact your soul.

-Sri Kaleshwar

It is just like Swami said, the experience of *Khandana Yoga* had a huge effect on my soul. It had lasting consequences I couldn't ignore.

One day, Swami casually mentioned that a magician came to Penukonda. The magician challenged Swami to prove that Swami was real. Swami accepted his challenge; it was on stage in front of lots of people. It was a spectacle designed to expose Swami as a fraud. Swami went on stage with a bird in his hands. He then broke the bird's neck, threw it down, and challenged the magician to bring it back to life! Of course, the magician couldn't do it. Then Swami did. The bird came back to life and flew away! Swami asked me, "Would you be interested in seeing that?" Of course, I said yes, I wanted to see that! This was an advanced yogic process called Khandana Yoga, which I had never heard of until then.

Soon after, a German student who had brought a small group to Penukonda began making a big fuss that Swami was going to kill a bird, and how terrible it was! By that time, Swami had announced he was going to do it. This student was going around saying how it wasn't right. I thought, 'If he is going to bring it back to life, why is there something wrong with that? Swami wanted to demonstrate a miracle and you are worried about the bird's life?' His concern seemed to be misplaced. I was also sure, given who Swami was, it was going to be of great benefit for the bird. Still, the guy went around talking to people about it. It seemed weird to me.

Swami spoke to a group of us and split us into two groups. We were going to be using a pigeon. There would be a group at his fire and a group with the pigeon. He would pick. He prohibited us from recording or photographing any high-energy process he did.

He called us late at night, after midnight. The people who went to the fire got some instructions. Then he asked different students if they would be willing to hold the knife. When someone said yes, he would say something to scare them. They had some fear and a judgment about whether it was right to do. He didn't ask me, probably because he knew I would say yes. He only asked those who had issues or fear.

Finally, somebody held the pigeon, while Swami used a serrated Indian kitchen knife and cut the neck. He was sawing his way through; it wasn't very elegant. He cut the neck and left a flap of skin holding the head to the body, and pretty much severed it. He had all of us get blood on our hands, holding the bird and draining some blood out of it. Everyone got blood on their hands. Clearly, the bird was dead.

He did this in front of the northeast of the Mandir. The people were sitting at the fire close by. Then we all walked to the fountain in the garden. The fountain hadn't been completed yet. Swami had the pigeon and stood on the edge of the fountain. He took off his scarf, dipped it in the water, wrapped it around the bird's neck, then blew on the scarf. Before we started, he pulled up his shirt sleeves to show there is nothing up his sleeves. Then he said, "Touch me." He was standing on the edge of the fountain, probably 18 inches higher than us. We all touched his feet. "No! Not my feet, touch me where I am touching the bird!" He said some mantras. I looked at his face and could see blue light coming out of his eyes. He was clearly altered. It was not a long time, maybe a minute. Then he unwrapped the scarf and the bird's head was back on! The bird wouldn't fly; it was the middle of the night and dark. But it was alive and whole again! Then someone took the bird and put it in a tree. In some ways, it didn't seem like a big deal. It was so natural. But the energy was really high and so heavy, and that blue light in Swami's eyes was exceptional.

Witnessing that had a profound effect on my soul. I received an enormous amount of energy from it. What was so unusual, after the process I would catch myself singing a song out loud! It was a *Talking Heads* song. I wouldn't consider myself a *Talking Heads* fan, but I would catch myself singing it and I didn't even know all the words. This happened many times over the days after this process. I thought, 'Why am I singing this?' It wasn't even a song I particularly liked. I didn't even know it. I had hundreds of music CDs and it was not one that I remembered. But the lyrics were so appropriate and were, for me, proof that

God had a sense of humor, and God knew me better than I knew myself. It showed me there was something remarkable going on with supernatural energy. I would be walking around singing verses of a song I didn't even know!

I had never been that happy, not in that way. Everything was the same, but everything was different. Something had changed in me like that. Some energy affected me deeply. There was no escaping that. What exactly happened to me, I couldn't say, but it was a profound change. I didn't talk to anyone about it. It was really shaking to my soul, not in a bad way. It's something you can't unsee or undo. Or explain away. Later some people asked me about my experience, and I said a little bit, but they dismissed it like it wasn't real. For me, the energy was so profound, my whole world had been shaken to the core, so I just stopped talking about it. I wouldn't talk about it with anyone, to talk about it would diminish it. Even if no one else understood it, I had to protect that in me.

Nityanandaji would talk about how Swami would do miracles for that exact reason – it stops our mind. That clearly did that to me. There was no cultural or logical reference for how that affected me. That happened very early on and was part of the reason that there was never any question about Swami for me, who he was, or what he could do. We have talked about people coming and being all enthusiastic, then one thing would happen, and they would be gone. For me, after that experience, I couldn't leave; I couldn't doubt.

Swami would never close the door if you wanted to doubt him, even with that, people would say that he switched birds, or did a trick, that it didn't happen. For me, what it came back to was the energy I felt and the experience I had. That energy was so clearly Divine, not of this world. I had no doubt. That whole thing about who was going to kill it was a big part too. Who could stand, who could he ask to do this and who would not go into fear?

If someone went into fear, it could crash the whole process. He would always do that, throw things out and watch people's reactions to see who was confident and who was shaky. He never asked me if I would cut it, I think he just knew that I wouldn't have any qualms about it. I wasn't enthused about killing things but for that I would have, especially knowing it would come back. I wasn't concerned about the karma of killing something.

With Khandana Yoga, you can't cut the head completely off, that is why he was careful about leaving it connected in a small way. I didn't know that until later. I was thinking I knew a better way to kill it. When I was a kid, I had to hold chickens when my grandfather chopped their heads off. My thing was, if you are going to kill it, make it fast and minimize the animal's suffering. I thought Swami could do it in a better way. That was coming out of my ignorance about what the process was. I didn't know until later, with a Khandana process you can't cut it completely off. I would have just whacked the head off thinking I was minimizing the bird's suffering, then I would have actually killed it! I learned that later because somebody did Khandana Yoga and cut the head off and their process crashed.

After the Khandana Yoga experience, I was in a state of bliss. But Swami would only let you stay in that state a short time so as not to get stuck but to keep going with your sadhana. The energy is in your soul bank account, to receive when the time is right.

Years earlier, I had seen the *Talking Heads* movie, *Stop Making Sense,* with the song I sang after the process. Mostly I watched the footage of them in concert, David Byrne with giant suits dancing around. A thing that struck me when watching them perform was to see how creative they were, and how much they were enjoying their lives. It made me realize there were people in the world who were doing things they really enjoyed, and I wasn't one of them. The movie made an impression on me. It was imaginative and unusual. I had never seen anything like it.

Home is where I want to be,
Pick me up and turn me around,
I feel numb, born with a weak heart,
I guess I must be having fun.
The less we say about it the better,
Make it up as we go along,
Feet on the ground, head in the sky,
It's okay, I know nothing's wrong, nothing.
Oh! I got plenty of time,
Oh! You got light in your eyes,
And you're standing here beside me,
I love the passing of time,
Never for money, always for love,

Cover up and say goodnight, say goodnight.
Home is where I want to be,
But I guess I'm already there,
I come home, she lifted up her wings.
I guess that this must be the place,
I can't tell one from the other,
Did I find you, or you find me?
There was a time before we were born,
If someone asks, this is where I'll be, where I'll be, Oh!
We drift in and out, Oh!
Sing into my mouth,
Out of all those kinds of people,
You got a face with a view.
I'm just an animal looking for a home and sharing the same space for a minute
    or two.
And you love me till my heart stops,
Love me till I'm dead,
Eyes that light up,
Eyes look through you,
Cover up the blank spots
Hit me on the head I got ooh!
    -David Byrne, *This Must be the Place*

Khandana Yoga Power Object

When my father passed, I inherited a pocketknife from him. It wasn't very expensive, but it was a nice knife. It was blue and had an inscription on it, 'Be the Light', which I thought was beautiful. I carried that knife in my kurta pocket all the time when I was in India. I used it for hanging flowers in Swami's office. In general, I kept it very sharp. One time, I was hanging jasmine flowers on the pictures in the living room when Swami saw the knife. He asked, "Is that knife sharp?" I told him yes. He asked for it, so I handed it to him. He quickly stabbed two holes in the cloth of the divan! He had a surprised look on his face then said, "It's sharp." Then, handed it back to me.

One evening I was walking from my apartment past the Dwarkamai to the Mandir when Swami stuck his head out and said, "I need a knife, get me a knife." He just stuck his head out; he didn't come out. That was an indication he was doing a process where he couldn't leave the building. I just happened to be walking by with a knife in my pocket. I showed him the knife and asked him if it would work. He took it. I had no idea who was in there or what was happening.

A day or two passed and the knife hadn't come back. I had an attachment to it because it was from my father. I had known that when I gave it to Swami it might not come back. I asked about it, then I found out that Nityanandaji had it. I went to Nityanandaji's room and asked him about it, and he gave it to me, but I could feel some reluctance. Sometime after, I asked him why he was reluctant to give it. He told me that it had been used in a process and it would be good to never lose it. Eventually, he told me that it had been used for Khandana Yoga. Once a knife is used for Khandana Yoga, it becomes a big power object, and can be used for that again. After that, I put it aside and stopped using it as my everyday knife.

Even though I was attached to it, once it became a power object I felt that it should be available to be used, so years later I gave it back to Nityanandaji. I felt he would be more likely than me to be able to use it again for a process.

Group of 11 in front of Badava Lingam, Hampi, 2001
Back row from right: Gustav Tillman, Terry, Virginia Grey, Mataji, Philip Lipetz, Paul
Aryeh, Myuri Zonka, Ramakrishna, Nancy Fengler, front row: Nityanandaji, Herbert

Badava Lingam

Swami with Group of 11, Tungabhadra River, Hampi, 2001

Group of 11 meditating, Tungabhadra River, Hampi, 2001

To Mother Divine Process, Hampi, 2001

Mother Divine Initiation, Hampi, January 1, 2001

Mataji, Mother Divine Initiation, Hampi, January 1, 2001

Terry, Mother Divine Initiation, Hampi, January 1, 2001

Teaching the Nine Arrows, Sri Sailam, 2002

Preparing to See Mother Divine

Here is my final advice: one type of happiness is to receive huge information. Raising up your energy, receiving a lot of shakti in your soul through meditation, that's one kind of real happiness. You must do the second one, practice meditation. If you have a hundred hours of information to listen to, and if you're not practicing that in two or three days, it's like putting the fragrance (perfume) in ash. Do you understand? Putting the fragrance in the ash — nothing. Only thinking, 'Why is Swami not with us, oooooh.' No. Just one word, one technique. Meditation. Do it. If for 365 days a year I keep on teaching without your practicing anything, nothing will happen. I want to teach how to ride a bicycle. You must climb on the bicycle; you must practice. Do you understand? Got my point? Done. It is very important. Practice.

-Sri Kaleshwar

In the early years, we did so much sadhana, easily 8 to 12 or 14 hours a day. Enormous amounts of japa. Swami created a group with 11 people, we went to the river every day and meditated for 7 hours a day. We meditated in the Dwarkamai for months, days on end doing nothing but japa and meditation! I was happy to do it. I really liked doing japa.

Before I met Swami, I had never done japa meditation, never repeated a mantra. The first time I met him, he gave us a mantra to do and I went into a deep trance. I had meditated for over ten years before that with no real experiences. Doing japa totally changed my perspective on meditation. I would have really deep, peaceful experiences. The silence was profound. I was kind of addicted to it! The more I did, the more I enjoyed it. I was mesmerized by it.

I had meditated for years with not much reward. Then Swami gave a simple mantra, and I had a profound experience. Whoo, this is the way it should have been all along! I would have been super excited to have done this for years. My meditation practice had been just plodding along, motivated more from obligation and a feeling that I needed to do it.

Starting with a new mantra can be challenging. For Westerners, they are unusual words in a foreign language. Swami stressed pronunciation was important so there was always some pressure to get it right. I would start with the mantra written on a piece of paper and try my best to say it correctly.

At first, it's difficult. But then as you progress to being able to say the mantra, the energy starts flowing. So that's usually some days or a week, and then at a certain point the mantra is just running in you, then you really feel the energy.

That whole process was such a new experience; it made such an impression on me. I had never had that experience of any meditation before meeting Swami. That experience was consistent with the different mantras he taught. Some are easier to learn, and quicker to get to the point where the energy is running. Once that happened, I would find that the mantra would be running in me without saying it. I could hear it in the background; it was going on automatically.

Doing japa all day was heaven for me. Probably because I could feel something happening and it was not difficult to do. I really enjoyed it. I'm one of those people that would have been happy to just sit under a tree and do japa.

Swami gave so much knowledge to us. It would take years of doing nothing else but sadhana to do every practice he gave. He gave so many techniques; you can choose the ones that resonate with you. Just the fact that you are doing something that he taught, he will respond to that!

Introducing Us to Mother Divine

Now I'm going to talk about Her structure. In the universe the most, the most, the most beautiful is She. But She pretends She is not beautiful. She pretends to be not beautiful.
-Sri Kaleshwar

At Christmas in 2000, Swami chose a group of men to visit a powerful ancient Kali Temple, which he said was for serious students. We all piled into the Ambassador cars and the drivers started driving. We had no idea where we were going. I thought it was somewhere nearby, but then we just kept driving for hours and hours. I don't know exactly how long we were driving, it seemed like six hours or so. I had to sit in the middle of the old Ambassador because I was too tall and would have hurt my neck.

Before reaching the temple, we stopped at a river to take a much-needed bath. We had a fresh set of clothes with us. The drivers drove into town and got us little packets of shampoo. We went in the river near the road and jumped in to take a bath, then put on a fresh set of clothes.

Then we went to the Kali Temple. It was very dark. The pujari brought us into the inner chamber. It was shocking how small it was: we barely fit. We weren't supposed to touch each other. We had to wiggle around to get a little room to sit and be as comfortable as possible. It was quite warm and humid. There were six guys. It was intense in there. Kali[19] was a little intimidating! I didn't have any fear, though. I knew enough already that if you are in front of God, fear is not a good thing.

It was the first time I saw a deity with silver teeth. The statue only had one tooth in, the *pujari* had to put the other tooth in. Kali's teeth curled way back into Her cheeks! We sat right next to Her. She was so dark, because it was very dark in the room, and She was black. I didn't see much detail. I saw Her arms but didn't focus there. I looked at Her face. When they put the silver covers on Her eyes, Her eyes really popped. It was something. That's what I focused on.

As soon as I sat down and got somewhat comfortable, I started the japa and immediately went into trance. It was a lot of energy, really heavy energy. I don't think it took me more than a minute. Then I would come back, look, and then again, go right back out into trance. I came out of trance when I realized there was something on my foot. It was a snake! I could feel it moving across me. Of course, well, we're in a Kali temple, it's probably a cobra. 'Okay, we're locked in this little room. What am I going to do?' I decided not to open my eyes. I didn't want to see it. It was not a little snake. I just kept meditating, and went right back into a trance, even with the feeling that the snake was there. Then the next time I came back, it was gone. Then when we were done, I came back to my body. I looked at Her again. By that time, I was suffering physically from being so cramped and the long car ride. We got up and wandered out. Everyone was altered.

After meditation, we walked around the temple and noticed sexual images carved on the roof. The roof was painted white; it was very distinct. Later I asked Swami about it, and he said most temples will have a sexual scene

---

[19] A statue of Mother Divine as a destroyer of negativity.

somewhere on them. In India, the union of God is understood to be sacred. It doesn't mean what it does in the West when you see something like that.

We drove back, and as soon as we arrived Swami had us in the Mandir in front of all the students. I don't think we even got a chance to clean up. He started asking us questions, even though before our journey he had told us not to talk about it, no matter what. I was sitting in the back, sweating bullets. I was terrified he was going to call on me.

After hearing the other students speak, I thought, 'Wow, they had profound experiences and I just felt a snake. I didn't see anything or hear anything.' Of course I felt the energy, but I was kind of intimidated by what they shared. But Swami didn't call me; he just switched and started talking about Mother Divine. I was really happy. He didn't call me! Maybe he knew I wasn't ready to talk about it. He picked on Nityanandaji, who shared some things very reluctantly after Swami's prodding. Then after sharing, Swami berated him for saying something, even though he was the one who asked him to talk! He grilled Ramakrishna, too. I was relieved he didn't ask me. With Swami, if he told you to do one thing, then said to go a different way, it was hard not to go that way. He was always tricky; you could never tell what he was going to do and what the right thing was in response. That trip, I learned to be much more careful about what I said. I started with the attitude of, I am not saying anything to anyone since I don't want to take a chance.

Until then, Swami had talked about connecting to angels. He had never talked about connecting to Mother Divine. This was a big switch. I'd seen traditional cultures worshipping the Mother, and had been involved in some that actually did, but this was a dramatic development in his teachings.

I am just now coming to understand that this process was the beginning of Swami's mission to connect all his students to the Divine Mother so that we could each have a relationship with Her.

Preparing for Mother Divine Darshan

Still the channels are available, and the doors are open for us from nature. This ancient divine knowledge is coming back again. If we follow that knowledge, we will have the results. My deeper aim is to connect everyone to Divine Mother... Once you experience Her energy, that energy is with you all the time. That energy purifies everything around you. Your soul turns as a divine soul...

Many people have seen Mother Divine and had a great experience. In the present situation, people can't believe it. "How is it really possible?" It's possible! It's possible! To recognize God, to see God, to communicate with God, to demonstrate miracles and give that experience to someone else, that is the ultimate research. That is the research of a soul scientist. That is the information written in the palm leaves. Every person can do it.

-Sri Kaleshwar

When Swami was teaching about the Divine Mother he asked the students, "What form of the Mother do you want to see? Beautiful or terrible?"

Some people wanted to see Kali as their first experience of Mother Divine. But for me, I knew that you can't be afraid when you see the Mother. For whatever reason, I felt that seeing Her would be enough without taking a chance of becoming fearful, so I wanted to see Her beautiful form. I was surprised that some people chose to see the terrible form. I think it was kind of a Western thing where people were trying to go to the extreme, or perhaps an exaggerated assessment of their soul capacity. I felt it would be better for me to do a gradual step before going for an intense experience. If you become fearful, you can die in darshan, literally have a heart attack! If you see a fierce form, you may not be able to hold that energy. It could crash you. Swami said it could be a life risk. He made it out to be a big deal; you had to be careful, aware, and humble.

That thing of wanting to see something intense, I didn't have that. If it really is that big, why would you even take a chance? That day in the temple, Swami looked at me when he asked people which form of the Mother they wanted to see. When he asked me, I said, "I want to see Her beautiful form. I want to be attracted, I want to see something that is striking and beautiful, not terrifying or scary." Maybe I had enough energy that I could see a terrifying form and handle it, but I wasn't sure, and I really didn't want to take a chance.

Swami was a dare and dash character. He always admired people, or at least seemed to, who were willing to risk everything on something. I never felt that way. When he asked me if I wanted to go fast or slow, I said slow. I would rather go slow with something that was sure rather than risk everything on a one-time win where I could lose everything. I think that was partially because I could stay in India indefinitely, so why hurry? He had commented before that other people came and could only stay for a certain time. Right from the beginning there was a time constraint and a restriction on what he could do with them. I was the opposite, since I knew I could stay longer I didn't see any reason to be in a hurry. I didn't know how long it would take or how hard it would be, but better to go incrementally than just jump to the highest. Different people had different ways of doing things, but that was my choice.

Preparing for Darshan

There were 11 of us that Swami put in a group to have Mother Divine's darshan. He sent us to do our meditations by the river in *Hampi*.[20] We did 12 hours a day of japa connecting to Mother Divine.

Swami put us through an intense process before we had darshan, to prepare us every angle. You've done so much purification, so much japa; he's run you through every emotion and whatever he could to prepare you beforehand, so you were really kind of wound up.

After about a month of meditation by the river, he called Mataji, Virginia, and I from out of the group to come to Penukonda for darshan. Swami then added three students who hadn't done any of the sadhana. It was a mix of advanced, middle, and beginning students. This was typical of Swami. He said the energy of advanced students automatically lifts the rest. He made efficient use of the energy; more people could benefit.

---

[20] Power spot in South India where Sri Kaleshwar taught and gave enlightenment processes to his students. Capital of the Vijayanagara Empire in the 14th century and mentioned in the Ramayana and the Puranas of Hinduism as Pampaa Devi Tirtha Kshetra.

The new group consisted of me and five women! They nominated me to be the group leader. As there was no permission to record Swami or take photos, one of the group who had just gotten out of college was chosen to take notes. We needed accurate notes of instructions and teachings Swami gave regarding our process.

Typically, there was a problem because people didn't agree on what he said. We would read the notes, and I would ask each person if they felt Swami had said something different. If needed, I would go and ask him for clarification. I would go even if I felt it was necessary only for the sake of the cohesion of the group and to make everyone comfortable.

The thing was, Swami was good about clarifying. He really wanted you to be clear, and the intention for the process had to be clear, and it was more than ok to ask for clarification. He spoke with Mataji and I about group cohesion and needing to keep the group on one page. We needed to work on keeping everyone working together in unity, which was sometimes difficult.

There were two people who always had a disagreement with what everyone else had heard. Mostly it was for them that I asked Swami for clarifications. They were both hard about things and had very fixed opinions different from the rest of the group. A few times I got frustrated, so as part of keeping the group cohesive, I didn't mind going to ask Swami questions. This was the first real time where I was forced to interact with him. Before that, when we would talk, it was because he came over, not because I went after him. It was a new thing for me to have to pull on him.

At first it was hard for me to track him down in the ashram. But when I found him, he was open and inviting. I would write the questions down beforehand and was clear about them. Swami would often be involved in something, which I became involved in. If he was eating, he would offer me food. Sometimes he wouldn't let me leave and started talking about all kinds of stuff. It was all interesting for me. He also brought up a bunch of emotions in me. The master is always purifying us. I had thought it would be simple, I would go ask him a question, he would answer, then I would go back to the group and report to them. But he didn't operate that way. It got trickier to interact with him, but it was pleasant. This is how I started interacting with Swami.

The way I think about it now, it was a good introduction to interacting with him. I didn't expect him to drop everything to talk to me. If he was in the swing, I would go near and hang around. I would watch if he was talking to other people. Normally he waved me over, he could feel if I had a question. I never felt like I was pulling on him. My sense was, he was impressed by how I interacted with him.

My Experience of Mother Divine

I went to the Mandir to ask Swami something. I was by myself, and he was coming down the stairs. He looked over and said, "Oh, hi darling." Swami had learned a new word. It was cute in an odd kind of way. I had never heard him say anything like that; it struck me as odd. Then he said, "Your group should come over." He gave some instructions and indicated that the darshan could happen soon.

Swami said something to me that popped my mind out, "She knows you better than you know yourself. She's waiting to see you. She wants to see you." She's waiting for us to get to the point where we can see Her. It's us who aren't looking. That was such a powerful statement to hear. She was waiting for me!

He told us to clean the Jesus Temple from top to bottom and prepare for the darshan that night. Later that evening, he had us sit in front of Jesus (the statue in the Jesus Temple), relax and make each other laugh. He wanted us to not be in our heads.

Sometime after, he told us to go downstairs to the Baba Temple where he gave us final instructions for seeing Her; not to talk to Her, not to look Her in the eyes, not to spend too much time because this was the first time. We had to go into the room, do *pranam*, ask Her for a boon and then leave. He also told what to ask Her for.

The darshan was to be in Swami's bedroom. We were all to wait in the waiting room until our turn, then go into the bedroom one at a time. Swami would be in the room with us.

I watched as each person came out of the room, they looked so altered. It was something. Finally, it was my turn. When I turned the corner to enter the room, I saw Her standing there smiling and waving to me! I was so surprised. It was such an inviting gesture! It melted me. She was beautiful, so incredibly beautiful. Her face was stunning. She was impeccable. Her brilliant sari was folded immaculately, completely what you would see in a goddess photo; the jewelry, the hair, everything. She matched my size; She didn't strike me as being too tall or too short. She was gorgeous! Like nothing I'd ever seen. I can't really describe Her. There is no beauty to compare with it. Because She was so alluring and beautiful, I was afraid to look at Her directly. I didn't want to be tempted to have any *kama* for Her. Instead, I immediately dived to pranam at Her feet. I pranamed but didn't touch Her feet. At Her feet, I closed my eyes and lost consciousness for some time. I felt like I was lost in eternity. Somehow, I am sure it was through Swami's grace, I brought myself back, got up, asked Her for a boon, thanked Her and said, "See you again soon, Mother."

We See Different Forms of Mother Divine

One of the instructions Swami gave the six of us was not to talk about our darshan with anyone, to be in silence and in the energy reflecting on the experience. To me, this wasn't difficult. It was easy. We had worked for months, even years, doing japa to reach the place where it could happen. And, the truth was, it was more natural and familiar than I expected. She is our Mother, so why wouldn't we feel that closeness with Her? Why wouldn't we feel that comfortable with Her? Her energy was huge, unbelievably strong, like nothing I had experienced before, but I didn't feel shaking inside since She seemed happy to see me. It wasn't at all terrifying. My mind was quiet, and my awareness was clear. I was struck by how inviting She was, waving and smiling; it was not scary at all.

After the experience, we were waiting in the Jesus Temple for Swami. Just then, one of our group came over to me and started describing her darshan, exactly everything Swami said not to talk about! I was trying to shoo her away without making it a big deal, trying not to lose touch with my experience which I was going over and replaying in my head. There she was just spilling everything. Finally, somebody in the group told her to be quiet. That's one of those things, when the energy gets high people can act really funny.

But it turns out, it was good that she shared with me. I learned that her experience was different from mine. Mother Divine looked completely different to her than to me. Everything she said was different from what I saw. Swami said that it was an experience unique to each person. Like *Vivekananda*,[21] he just saw Her big toe. For me, I clearly saw Her, the whole form.

Although I was a little irked by her sharing, I did learn that it really was an individual experience the Mother tailors to each person. She knows you more than you know yourself. She knows what you need. It was amazing to realize that each time a person entered the room, they saw a different embodiment of the Divine Mother.

Swami talked about Mataji's experience and was super happy about it. In Mataji's darshan, Mother Divine put Her foot on Mataji's head. Swami told us he had never seen that before. It had only happened to one other person in history. It was a super great symptom. He was really happy with the way it went. Really happy. Swami's only real happiness was the success of his students. He was happier for us than we were ourselves because he knew the depth of what Mother Divine was giving us.

If you are born on this planet, you have the right to know Mother Divine. She's been waiting to see you your whole life. She wants to see you more than you want to see Her.

---

[21] (January 12, 1863 to July 14, 1902).

Kanaka Durga, Penukonda

After Darshan

Once you see Her, then you're a completely different person. You know something. You recognize unbelievable greatness in nature. Then you won't care about this world. Even though you're involved with a part of your soul with this planet, a part is always with Her. That's very important. That's very important.

-Sri Kaleshwar

After our darshan with Mother Divine, we were informed that we had to pack and leave for Hampi right away. All of us were looking forward to sleeping and savoring our experience. Instead, we had to pack and drive on a long road trip to Hampi. Within hours of having the Divine Mother's darshan, we were on the road. The rest of the students in the group of 11 were already there. I ended up in a room with Ramakrishna and Nityanandaji. It was very strange to be with them, I was unbelievably altered. The good thing is, because we showed up so soon after everyone else, most people assumed nothing happened.

After darshan, our small group all faced challenges. Two of the women's husbands were jealous and felt that they should have been the ones to have that experience and were quite put out by it. I had an interaction with a student who figured out what had happened, he had been told he was supposed to be in our group and then something happened that prevented it. It wasn't a huge thing, but it was someone I felt very close to, and I was surprised how hard he took it. I said some things to try to help but wasn't very successful.

I was sensitive about everything. Often, I can just walk into a room and feel the energy. That sense was amplified now, so being around other students' jealousy was hard. As I was not quite back, normal things that probably wouldn't have bothered me did bother me. It took months to digest that experience. It was life-changing. In some ways I adjusted, but it was a high point in my life. That sensitivity or that newness took time to adjust to.

Our little darshan group of six got tight; we didn't want to interact with others, we would have been much happier to just be together and not talk to anyone else. Fortunately, no one tried to ask direct questions. Because of this, our little group kept meeting and spending time together. It was almost like I couldn't relate to anyone else except the group; it was such a major shift in my consciousness. Aside from the hurt feelings and jealousy of others, it was just difficult for all of us to relate to anyone else. I was extremely altered. Everything was odd, I would say almost like I was on a psychedelic trip. We were in the hotel and one of us literally walked into a glass door. She dropped her keys, picked them up and went on like nothing happened. Mataji wore her clothes inside out and didn't notice. I was not the only one that was off!

That lasted for some time. It was profound. The first time I experienced that level of alteration was during the Khandana Yoga experience. With Mother's darshan it was different, and it took a lot of time to integrate what had happened.

After a short time in Hampi, Swami brought our group back to Penukonda, and announced he was going to send me to a Kali Temple, and I was going to stay there all night. I was still reeling from darshan and didn't think I was ready, but said, "If you think I am ready, I will do it." Of course, Swami played it up, stoking the fire. "You are going to be alone in the dark in the Kali Temple, late at night." He told me that I would be going in one or two days. I had some time to prepare but She could show up anytime! Also, just because I was there didn't mean She would appear.

It was evening the next day. Somebody was going to drive me over there, get me into the temple, then lock me in. I did all the preparation. I was sitting in the Mandir waiting. I had a little bag with water and a towel. Then Swami came in and checked me over, assessing if I was ready, then said, "Not today." I never heard any more about it.

I felt like it was a test to see if I would do what he asked, despite how frightening it sounded. On my part, if he said I was ready and believed it was the right thing then I was going to do it. I saw Mataji before I went over to the Mandir, and she was so surprised that I was going to be in that temple all by myself. One thing I know is, you can't have fear. If you see Kali and are afraid, it will escalate. I can say I didn't feel overly confident, but I didn't feel fearful either. I also knew it could be a life risk, if you suck fear then it could be over. Kali can appear terrifying, but She is not. She is destroying negativity, not creating it. Kali's sword has a bulge at the end; that kind of sword is made for beheading. You usually see Her with that sword holding a severed head. Around Her waist is a skirt of left hands, she cuts off the left arm at the elbow and has a skirt of unclean hands representing Her chopping off the negative actions we have done.

We had a *diksha* after our darshan that none of our blood could drop on the ground. You couldn't step on a piece of glass and bleed on the ground, or it stopped your process. For me, the *maya* hit with three completely different incidents, three days in a row. First, I cut my foot outside doing pradakshina around the Mandir. Second, I was taking care of an instrument of Swami's, when suddenly it penetrated my finger and I bled on the ground. Third, I was walking down the stairs and a nail poked through my plastic shoe and I bled on the ground. Three different things, three days in a row. It was incredible.

Of course, I was freaked out about it because Swami had given us the diksha and three days in a row, different things hit me, and I broke the diksha. I couldn't believe it. I had never bled on the ground before; that had never happened! I didn't want to tell him, but I knew I had to. When I did tell him, he started smiling. It was a good thing! He told me he gave that diksha specifically to see who the Mother would pick, so it was a good indication.

Swami had asked me how I wanted my spiritual process to go, if I wanted to go really fast and bet everything on one experience. You can go fast, but you have to be able to handle it. I said, "Absolutely not, I want to go slow and sure. I do not want to go fast." My feeling was that qualified me for a one-shot deal without knowing it because that's what he did with me. He made sure I didn't know, which is why he stopped doing processes with me. Why? Because I was done. I just didn't know. Then he had me do *seva*. Why? Because seva would keep me busy while I recognized what I had received. It's one of those things you don't recognize. You don't recognize your own energy; you don't know what you are carrying.

I'm not a big gambler. I wasn't willing to risk everything in one process. I didn't want to do that. I felt I had time and didn't need to be in a hurry. I felt I better go incrementally than to try and leap over the whole process. Except that's exactly what he did. He had brought me to Mother directly.

Satsang: Approaching Mother Divine

Mataji and Terry, Divine Mother Center, 2018

Mataji: We do japa and meditation to quiet the mind and receive energy, shakti. This enables us to stand in Her presence during darshan. The most important thing is to have control of your mind and be in *sthita pragnata* as much as possible. Her energy is the most powerful in creation; we need to have strict boundaries on our minds.

Terry: Of all these things, doing japa, building your energy, and silence. It's a huge refuge.

Mataji: Developing deep silence is the way to approach the Divine Mother. Then you will not be shaky in Her presence, your mind and communication with Her will be clear.

Terry: And an open heart, a surrendered and open heart, open to what She brings or gives you, then to integrate that into your life.

Mataji: Integrating the energy we receive from Mother Divine can take a long time. The experience changes you forever, everything is different after seeing Her. You are fundamentally different. It's very hard to put into words. It's like walking through a door into another reality, yet still being in this one. It continues to grow. You receive knowledge that teaches you about the Mother, and the creation. She constantly downloads knowledge into your consciousness.

Terry: For me, that information comes in silence. You must have some control of your mind, that it's not racing, that it's not roaring, that it's quiet enough to hear. Maintaining silence to be able to hear that information. Swami prepared me for that with the Mother. Swami could tell me something out loud, but mostly he would speak to me in the silence. I could hear him, not his voice, but something I would just know to do, and if I did that, it would be the right thing. You figure that out by trying it, by doing it, then seeing if it was the right thing.

Then the next time you know and listen to it. Swami was always upping the ante, like saying, 'Now can you hear this?'

Mataji: Yes, the master is looking to see if we caught the ball. The master is always throwing the ball seeing if you can catch it. Training us. Baba said there were three types of disciples: the first, the ordinary disciple, the master tells you to do something, and you do it when you get around to it. The second, is the average student, when the master tells you to do something, you do it. The third kind, the advanced student, the master doesn't have to say anything, the student does it before the master asks for it.

Terry: I was in between all three all the time! Swami, often if he had to say it, you already missed it. If I have to tell you, it's too late. Often, I felt that. If he had to say it, I already blew it! It was that training of listening in the silence. Our communication was mostly non-verbal. One example, I have always carried a knife in my pocket, even in Penukonda. Like when someone needed to open a box, he just looked at me and moved his eyes, like, 'Go help them.' He was in front of a group and talking. I would not walk in front of everyone, but once he looked, I knew that I had his permission to go and help. He looked at me and moved his eyes, I knew what he was saying. A simple example. If you were looking someplace else, you could miss it.

Getting a Personal Power Spot

One night Swami called me over to the dhuni. He told me to do a process, meditating for some hours with a little tin. Then I had to bury it on the grounds where I would know exactly where it was. I had to do it before morning. I picked a place between a wall and a tree and buried it.

Then Swami started building the Dwarkamai. When it was finished, he held a ground-breaking ceremony. He said it would be a special place where miracle energy would happen. Politicians and other important people came. When it was over, I was standing there when Swami looked at me and said, "Get a shovel and dig." I got a shovel and dug a little bit. "You have no idea how important this is," he said.

Soon after, Swami talked about power spots for the first time, then did this same process with the tins with everyone else. The power spots were going in the Dwarkamai.

He told me to do it again. We had gotten the clay from the earth around the *Badava Lingam* in Hampi, which we were to put in a tin, charge with our personal mantras, and bury.

For some reason, I can't remember why now, when the time came to complete the process, we had to bury the tin in the Dwarkamai but didn't have any of the special earth for my tin. When I told Swami, he took his big toe, stepped on the ground, and said, "Use that." I picked up his toe print and put it in my tin. That is what is in my tin in the Dwarkamai. My tin has Swami's toe print.

The Promise

My commitment to Swami began after our Mother Divine experience. I was in the Baba temple one night and Swami came up and started talking to me. He said I had won his heart. Then, "You need to take care of me as long as I am alive." He asked for my commitment. His commitment was to take care of me as long as I was alive. It wasn't just one way. He made me promise to take care of him, and he promised to take care of me.

Since the very first time I met Swami, he had been talking about taking off, taking *mahasamadhi*. So, I thought, well, he probably won't be around that long; this commitment probably won't be too difficult or long since he'll take off soon. I took it very seriously, but I truly believed it would not be for that long. In that same conversation, he also told me he was going to turn avadhut in the future. He said it like it was a big deal. I had no idea what that meant. I had heard the word, but my understanding of what it meant was very limited. I had a vague image of a saint who could manifest rocks and throw them at people to run them off, as someone with some amusingly anti-social behaviors.

At the time, I had no idea of the significance of our conversation. After he told me that I won his heart, he asked me what I wanted. My feeling was, 'If you are who I believe you are, I don't need to tell you what I want. I want what's best. You know better, I don't know what I am qualified for. I don't know what the best thing would be to ask for.' These thoughts were going through my head, and that I might ask for something stupid or something that was not in my long-term best interest. Then I basically told him, you know what is best for me. I wanted what he wanted for me.

I believe even then he knew he would have me as his attendant, and that he knew the direction things were going. I was a willing participant. I said yes with no hesitation. At that time Swami was still quite soft and sattvic. Later, he became very avadhut. If I would have seen that first, I might have thought about it more. Years later, it turned out to be difficult to be around the avadhut energy. At that time, I had no idea what taking care of an avadhut meant. The avadhut part especially. But I had already read about Shirdi Baba, and I knew that serving the master was the only sadhana Baba did. One of the highest things a master can give a student is to serve him.

One evening, I was on security in the Jesus Temple sitting near the office door. Swami came out and went to Jesus. There is a beautiful statue of Jesus that he would pray to every morning. He was doing something there with Jesus, it was late at night and the lights were low so I could not see. It was after midnight on the day of my birthday. He was doing something, moving his hand; he might have been manifesting it. Then he dropped it. It was a gold ring with a diamond. He told me, "This is from Jesus." He said he was giving it to me because I was a real diamond in his life.

Mother Divine Process with Swami, 2002

Mother Divine Process with Swami, 2002

Mother Divine Process with Swami, 2002

Mother Divine Process with Swami, 2002

Jesus Temple

Jesus Murthi

The Jesus Miracle

For example, a few people[22] are doing the channelings with Jesus. They're touching the Jesus statue to make him bleed. I gave a channel. They're locking the door, they're lighting the candles, they're touching Jesus' heart doing their process and process and process. They're pretty close, almost 99.99% close. What type of energy it is? Is it their energy, the Mother Divine energy, the Jesus energy, their master's blessings, or they cut off the illusions and their heart is melting? You have to search the points. You have to dig the points. Is it their self-energy; or from what they practiced for many years, they're bringing that cosmic energy out and doing it? Or is it coming from Mother Divine? Where? They practiced for many years with a pure open heart. Sadhana means real pure dedication.

-Sri Kaleshwar

Soon after our group had been through the process of darshan with Mother Divine, Swami told us we needed to demonstrate and prove the energy we had received from the Divine Mother. Our next process was for us to enliven the Jesus statue. The Jesus Temple was above the Baba Mandir; it was also where Swami lived. His private quarters, his meeting place and office were located there. He had recently finished constructing the temple and gotten the Jesus statue.

Our group of five women, including Mataji, and me, went to the Jesus Temple to do a process. In that process, each of us had to go up and touch Jesus' heart; we had mantras and things to do. The funny thing was, we would each go up to touch Jesus for the same amount of time, but some disagreements arose about who got to touch Jesus longer! This is the kind of thing that would happen in a process, suddenly people start behaving funny, but you have no choice other than to work it out. When the energy goes high, people go funny, guaranteed!

So, we decided I would set my watch, which had a stopwatch. I was in charge. The part you have to understand is, it was a Jesus process. The Jesus energy is super thick, unbelievably heavy. I had the watch in my hand, and all I

_____

[22] The Mother Divine darshan group of six.

had to do was push a button. But in the time it took someone to walk up to Jesus, I would trance out! The timer didn't do any good if I didn't push the button. I would come back to awareness but had no idea how long it had been! Nobody realized that I wasn't paying any attention; I could not tell if I had passed out for one second or ten minutes. So, I would just push the button. It was an indication of the energy that was part of this process.

Swami had said it would take some time for the process to happen. Every day for hours, we were doing our process in the Jesus Temple. Swami would walk every day during that time and was monitoring us very closely. After some weeks, he told us to sit near his northeast bed, then told us we were failures. Our groupism wasn't good enough and we weren't generating enough energy! It wasn't obvious to everyone, but he was testing us.

One thing about Swami, he could convince you that the sky was green. After a few minutes, you would agree with anything he said. So, the idea that our group was a failure, we kind of believed that. He gave us a choice; he could do the process for us, or we could keep trying. And we could choose a different substance, an easier one. We had a choice of oil, blood, or *amrutha*. We chose blood because it was the highest shakti. We went for the highest. "Maybe you want to choose the oil instead?" We said no. He told others publicly, not to us, "I was testing them to see how much they will stand." Do you have the same dedication even though you get punched and get sidelined by something? Not just dedication, but inspiration and confidence. When Swami punched like that, it shakes your confidence and generally you go down. That's part of the training, to see how you get back up from that. We decided that we wanted more time to continue, and we were sticking with our choice of blood.

Then some days later, he called and said we were doing the process that night. We were to clean the entire Jesus Temple, the altars, put flowers and candles, and make it beautiful and sparkling. My experience in these processes was we did spiritual practices for a time, sometimes a long time, sometimes a short, at the right time, he would call us for the culmination of that experience. It was always a struggle before that, things would come up, but once the culmination was happening, suddenly, the bliss would start – immense happiness and bliss. It was just fun. We had done the hard work, and at the end, we got the reward, the result of the process. You don't have a chance unless you have persisted and have done the hard work and stood in the testings. But after that, it is fun! The energy was so beautiful and joyous. We were so happy. We knew something special was going to happen. You knew Swami was going to do something great, and you were just in this buoyant mood.

After doing our process with Jesus, he told everyone but Mataji and I to close their eyes, turn around and not look. Then Swami, Mataji, and I watched as the blood flowed from Jesus down onto the floor! It was incredible, it just continued to flow from the feet of Jesus! A third of the temple floor had become filled with Jesus' blood! Jesus' presence, his love, the highest shakti, was released in that blood that just spread out before our eyes! The energy was so high it was hard to contain. There was so much love. The energy was still heavy and thick. It was shocking in the most beautiful way. Later, Swami shared that it was the highest Shiva energy he had experienced in his life.

Being in a process with Swami not only gave a direct experience of the Divine, but gave a glimpse of his real greatness. It was incredible to be in a divine process with him and see him in action. He was not the same person as when he was in the energy. He was a 'high professional' in the energy channels. That's why a lot of saints would come asking his help to see Mother Divine even though he was not even 30 years old. He was the high-professional and could handle Kali energy.

That's how the Jesus statue got enlivened, and how Jesus' blood came to bless the Jesus statue.

The Significance of Blood
(Mataji's comments at La Verna, Italy, 2019, where St. Francis first received the stigmata)

We are here where St. Francis first received the stigmata. Blood is a big theme in Jesus' life; Jesus' blood is holy. The teachings of the ancient knowledge say the blood, flesh, and bones of saints are holy. Blood carries a soul's power and a divine soul's blood carries the highest power, the highest shakti, blessings and purification. The spilling of holy blood is a huge energetic transmission into the creation. Most especially, Jesus' blood.

We see the theme of blood with Christian saints. Many Christian saints, male and female, have received the stigmata. During communion, Catholics are symbolically drinking Jesus' blood and eating Jesus' flesh. The Eucharist and wine are symbols of Jesus' flesh and blood.

Swami shared during a darshan with Jesus that Jesus held his hand. After the darshan, Swami showed his hand which had a burn mark. "See, even me," he said, "has to go through purification. That is Jesus!"

PART THREE:
HUMAN & DIVINE

Human Face of Divinity

We do not know the different kinds of saints, how they behave, what they do, what they eat. We only know that through God's grace they manifest themselves in this world to liberate the ignorant and bound souls. If there is a store of merit in our account, we have a desire to listen to the stories and leelas of the saints, otherwise not.
-Sri Sai Satcharitra.

I could see Swami's divinity and I could see Swami's human side. I didn't put him on a pedestal, but I didn't treat him as a friend either. I had that attitude from the start. Very seldom would Swami and I hang out and chat. That wasn't our relationship like it was with some other students. Even though he interacted with the world in a normal way, he was not a normal character. For me, it was always important to never lose sight of that. I wanted to stay on that level in all my interactions with him. I never wanted to lose that perspective of who he really was while having proximity. For me it was a question of respect. That's also why I never questioned what he did. I didn't know why he did things the way he did, but you could see the results. They spoke for themselves.

Swami always said that he was not a god, and we should not worship the guru as a god. We should have respect and gratitude for the master as a friend, not worship him. He said that there was no difference between us except he knew certain things that we didn't know.

Swami showed us the human face of divinity. He suffered the same things we did; he had headaches, he got sick, had family problems, had political problems, etc. It was part of being human, he said. He shared his life brutally honestly with those close to him. He wanted to demonstrate that an enlightened master was also a human being. He wanted us to share his personal life with the world so people would see the reality, setting them free from their faulty notions of enlightenment.

Swami also showed the reality of how a supernatural person with miracle abilities operates in this creation. He had the ability to see the future. He could see what was going to happen. But he begged Baba to close it down. He told me, "Don't ever ask for that, then you know who's going to betray you, everything!"

Mostly we have romantic ideas of what supernatural abilities are like. The reality is very different. A well-known author came to Swami and asked to be given every supernatural power. Swami looked at him and said, "Are you crazy? You don't want that!"

Responsibility comes with each of these things. How much are you going to sacrifice of yourself? Swami was very happy to be on his own; he was in his bliss. He sacrificed that to be with people and deal with our problems. He took on our karmas. As soon as he interacted with any of us, he was handling our illusions and taking them on. If he works with a couple, their illusions are flowing on him, both the husband and the wife will have their reactions to what he is saying. It is amazing to me that he was willing to sacrifice that way.

The Guru's Tests and Leelas

Then he (the Guru) took me to a well, tied my feet with a rope and hung me from a nearby tree upside down by my feet! I was suspended three feet above the water, which I could not reach with my hands, nor could I drink with my mouth. After suspending me like this, he went away, and no one knew where. After four or five hours he returned, quickly removed me, and asked how I fared. 'In bliss supreme. How can a fool like me describe the joy I experienced?' I replied.

-Sri Sai Satcharitra

When I first went to the ashram, Swami spent a lot of personal time with me. I never expected it, but it happened. Then later, he told me the program was coming and he was going to be busy, and he might not talk to me for a while. It was a year before he talked to me again in private. Sometimes he would say something in a program, but nothing to me personally for that entire year. It was a little pinching, but it wasn't too bad since I had never held an expectation that I had to interact with him.

Before going on duty permanently to serve him, he began checking to see how I would handle things. He was testing to see what I would do. Around that time, Swami had bought a farm. One day he announced, "Tomorrow, Terry's going to go to the farm with me." Some people made a big deal out of it. Oh, you get to go to the farm; we never get to go. The next morning, I went to the Mandir and waited. Pretty soon it was lunchtime, then evening and not a peep. I just sat on the Mandir steps. Finally, one of the Indian staff came and said, "You are not going today." I thought it would have been nice if somebody told me instead of sitting outside the Mandir all day, but I didn't get upset about it. Swami liked to test people's patience and see how they handle not getting something they were told they were going to.

At one point, Swami started charging rent for rooms, and charged me double! I asked the person who was collecting the rent, "Why am I paying double?" She said it was because of Swami. I didn't say anything about it. He charged me double for more than a year. Then that woman asked Swami again, "Can Terry's rent go back down?" His response was, "Did he ask for that?"

Fortunately, I had not. My feeling was if I had said anything, it would have gone up four times! If you feel you are owed something, or something is unfair that the master is doing, you are damaging your relationship with your master. I am convinced if I would have asked for a reduction it would have gone up. You have to be careful how you approach the master. He has a reason which you don't know. I was happy to pay. He asked for it, so I paid without complaining.

Swami gave me another test, which was quite unusual. He told me he wanted to check if I knew the *Gayatri* mantra, I said yes. He said, "I want you to meditate for one hour on the *Gayatri* exactly." He said I had to go where nobody was around, where I could be by myself, and no one could disturb me. I didn't know where to go, but he said to start right away and meditate for one hour exactly. I had to look around to find a place immediately.

I found a place in a little stairwell closet. I put a cushion down, went in there, closed the door, and started meditating. After about 45 minutes I heard some commotion, somebody looking for me! Swami had told me to meditate for exactly one hour and not get disturbed. He had said it a couple of times, he made the diksha quite clear to me. Even though they were looking for me, I knew I had to do what he said. Eventually, I heard his voice calling me too, not too close but I could hear him. I was not going to come out before one hour! After the hour was up, I came out and everyone was asking me where I was and were all upset. Swami was getting ready to go and was looking for you!

One day, Swami kept saying to everyone that he was going to put me to work in his office. I just laughed every time he said it. I thought he was joking. It was pretty funny. I am a construction worker. There were professional personal assistants who knew how to use a computer, who knew how to type. I do not have any of those skills. I thought I was safe. I didn't believe he would really put me in the office.

But then he did. Not only me, but another guy, Thomas, who was almost as unqualified as me. The first day we just sat in the office. Thomas knew how to use the computer a little and knew how to type with two fingers, but that was two more than me. I didn't even know how to use the fax machine. I thought, well, at least I can keep the power going. At that time, we used a crude UPS to keep the electrical power going. I thought, I can do that, I can make sure the power keeps going. But correspondence, typing, anything else, forget it.

The first day in the office, Swami sent one of his Indian staff to give us a message. He told us that Swami said, "You have to wear your underwear today. Take all your clothes off and just be in the office in your underwear!"

"What??!!"

We immediately went out to talk to Swami who was sitting in his swing. We asked about the message. "Swami, one of the staff told us that we have to wear our underwear. Why is this? Why do we have to do this?"

"You didn't thank me!" he said. He was serious! He wasn't serious about the underwear, but he was like...you didn't thank me! He made the point that he was taking care of us, and we didn't acknowledge it. I was really surprised. I can say, I was shocked that he put me in the administration office to begin with. I just couldn't believe I was in the office; running the ashram was a big deal.

But after some months, we acclimated and somehow worked out our systems and it got easier and easier. That was the way that Swami taught, he just threw you in the deep end, and you had to learn to swim.

After six months or so, just as we were feeling confident, Swami took us out of the office!

Satsang: Being Ignored

Swami and students, Penukonda Ashram, 1999

SWAMI: Suppose I gave Virginia too much love and happiness. Suppose I gave too much love to Nancy, and she can't handle it properly. Suppose you can't handle it properly... how we say that? Your emotions are not being maintained properly about simple things, important things, very important things, very less important things. Taking power, the energy from the master. Then the master thinks, "Uh-huh, no way." The master thinks, "Why waste my time?" The real divine energy students must handle it, like Terry, 100% true, just 100% is like that. Did anybody observe him asking Swami a question anytime, anywhere?

Virginia: He doesn't.

SWAMI: Never! But he has a lot of questions, but he is getting answers himself. He been through a very hard time emotionally, is it true?

Terry: Yes.

SWAMI: Very, very hard time he been through. Emotionally, completely purifying himself. I'm simply watching and I'm laughing to myself, he's doing his thing, putting his chair there. Sometimes he's walking, sometimes he's upstairs, but I never talk to him for even five minutes, "Ok, come Terry, how you're doing?" Just I'm looking and I'm ignoring him, is it true?

Terry: Um-huh.

SWAMI: Just ignoring him. Even sometimes I say hi to my dogs, I play at least one or two minutes with my dogs sometimes, but I didn't with him. He had complete patience, waiting, and doing himself. I'm not insulting the students, but it's important to handle as much as you can to spiritually progress and grow. Everyday a person must recognize how much they learned that day. 'What new information did I learn? How many hours did I meditate? How much vibration did I receive? How much power did I receive? How much peace did I enjoy? How much time was I in the divine energy?' They must recognize it themselves, and only they can. Every day when I lay down, I review from early morning until night, everything I said, what I did, what new information I learned, what I learned from my students, how they're behaving, what are their emotions, what I advised them, what I'm doing on the construction site, the inner side, what I am doing on the administration side – everything in ten minutes. It's very, very important.

The master always observes each step, point-to-point knowing how his students are doing. Is the master driving the students crazy or are the students driving the master crazy? Everybody thinks, 'Oh, master is driving the students so crazy,' that's never true. When the students are driving the master crazy, then he steps back a level for protection. 'Hey, why I should go very near to them? It's not necessary to teach the secret information. It's not necessary to teach them the secret, secret powerful things because they're so wild and crazy about little things. They don't have simple control of their emotions. If they had huge powers, completely they would misuse them, they don't know how to handle it.' It's like giving a five-year-old kid a Mercedes Benz car to drive but he's only fit for the small car toy in the house. It means his mind only has certain boundaries. The master keeps trying to extend his boundaries, but if it's not happening – forget it. The master can jump out.

Satsang: Testing My Patience

Swami and students, Penukonda, 1999

SWAMI: Don't be responsible for negative karma. You can't recognize it now, but one day you'll recognize the value of positive karma, 100%. It's a promise. You will recognize how negative karma really affects and ruins your life. It will come up; it will react on you. You have to purify your soul from the beginning when it created the negative karma. You have the best period in the master's presence to purify it. You can hook him, the master's heart, easily with your love. Why am I only able to speak to a couple of people, not the remaining people, is because of their hearts. They really want to talk to Swami and they're completely open. They want to talk, they want to talk, they want to talk. Automatically, their magnetic power brings them, then I say, "Hey come, sit, talk a little while." You know what I mean?

Sometimes I push a little and give some pressure to make them stay a little away. How much you come forcefully, is how much you're in the illusions. When the master is ready, but he's not talking to you, he's not looking to you, he's not caring about you, but you're doing such great meditations, you're really doing *abhishek*, you're doing unbelievable sadhana, but he's not focusing at all on you. What type of illusion is around you? Can anybody say? Ramakrishna?

Ramakrishna: Can they tell what type of illusions are around?

SWAMI: Uhm hmm.

Ramakrishna: Not if you're in the illusion! (laughing). I don't understand exactly what the question is.

SWAMI: Gosh, do you understand the question, Terry? For example, one year back, was Swami talking to you fluently (a lot)?

Terry: When I first came you talked to me a lot.

SWAMI: First, then later?

Terry: No.

SWAMI: How much time gap did I give?

Terry: Well, you just started talking to me now!

Ramakrishna: Two years, two and a half years.

SWAMI: 100% I did it purposely. He was watching and sitting. How much patience do you really have? How much he can really stand (with whatever is happening)? What can his soul dharma do here? He won it, completely I failed! (laughter). To be honest, I failed, he won it. I want that from my students. I want failure, or my students won't get success! I'm happy about that. Hey, if your teacher, if his students get really good marks, if the student is going up, the master feels so happy. Who planted the seed, if the tree is growing, the farmer says, "Wow, oooh!" The farmer always feels so happy. The teacher says, "Great, grow, learn."

Testing on the Ancient Knowledge

Swami was serious about all kinds of testing. In 2000, Swami gave all the students an actual test. It was on most of the knowledge that would eventually become the *Sai Shakti Healing* book. Swami always used an opportunity to strike as many targets as possible. In this instance, he said the people who didn't pass would have to go home! I didn't know if he would do that, but he sure made a big deal about it. Of course, it did make everyone really study. The master must push you harder than you push yourself. He was strict about knowledge. He demanded people study and contemplate it, and most of all, maintain its integrity, not pollute it with their own ideas. The guru can give many things, he can teach knowledge, but he cannot transfer it. It has to come through your hard work, study, and dedication. Most of all, he wanted people to be empowered. Knowledge is the ultimate empowerment; it cannot be taken away from you. Also, without people understanding the knowledge, he couldn't go deeper. I got the message.

I studied a lot before the test. I had recordings of all his talks, so I listened and reviewed my notes. In school, I was never that interested so mostly I didn't do that well. But like I said, I really was serious as a student when I went to the ashram. If he was teaching a specific healing technique, I would write which disk it was on and the minutes where he was talking about it, so I could review and listen to his actual words on the technique. It was a big deal because there really was a huge amount of information to learn, a lot of techniques, a lot of mantras and in-depth philosophy.

Some days later, after midnight, he called everyone to the Mandir and gave out the questions. I finished at sunrise. It was pages and pages, a huge number of techniques, mantras, essays, everything. I knew that I wouldn't remember the mantras very well, but the general concepts and specifics of the techniques I felt like I understood. I don't remember what score I got but I was happy with how I did. I couldn't have cared less that I didn't get a perfect score! Who cares, I passed!

Later, Swami gave another test. By the time he gave this one, I was working in the office and didn't have much time to study. He did all the same things, telling us if you didn't pass you had to go home! There was a big fear and anxiety about the test. I knew I wouldn't do as well as before because I just didn't have the time to study.

It took about nine hours for people to complete that exam. That's how serious Swami was. And it was Swami who graded those tests by putting his hands on the test and giving a score. That really created a lot of reactions in people, but not for me. My score was two points above failure, over the cut-off point for getting sent home! Later, Swami made a big deal about how I barely made it. I just looked at him and said, "I made it, that's all that counts!"

For me, it didn't bother me that I didn't get a perfect score. I was happy to have passed. If I had an idea that it had to be perfect, it could have really gotten to me, but it didn't. I passed. And for how little I got to study, I was happy with that. But it hooked a lot of people, another opportunity for a lot of ego washing.

Swami was serious about tests because he was serious about learning the knowledge. He wanted to see what people understood. Swami's teaching style was unique, he would discuss the highest spiritual subjects but not in a linear way. It required serious study and reflection. It became clear to him who really did that work with the dedication required.

More Relationship Leelas

In my personal life, I had finally adjusted to being married. Then suddenly one day, Swami started to mention that he could see we were not doing well. He began planting seeds that the relationship wasn't good for me. I started questioning the relationship, not seeing how it could work.

One day Swami took me aside and said, "You need to divorce her." I was shocked. He asked me if I wanted to do it on the phone, in person, or write a letter. It was my worst nightmare. He handed me the phone and told me to call her right away. At that time, there were no phones in the ashram, so I had to use his cordless landline.

I called and got her answering machine and left a message that I needed to talk to her. A couple of days later, she called Swami's number, so they ran around the ashram to find me. I told her things weren't working, and we needed to end the relationship. She was devastated. I really wasn't happy about the whole thing and I hadn't wanted to get married in the first place!

I had to give Swami his phone back. He was in his swing and was happy and excited. He said, "You don't know how good this is! The last day of *Navaratri*, this is Baba's samadhi day! It's an auspicious day. You did it, everything is good." Swami told me I could never go back. I was a little surprised because I wasn't thinking about going back.

Later, he closed the ashram and everyone had to leave. I was the only Westerner in the ashram. He told everyone in a public talk that I was going to oversee the construction of the Jesus Temple. He had me draw a little sketch of how the temple would look that I was going to oversee. I walked around with him a couple of times. That was the extent of my construction work. He told me later he had said that so I wouldn't go back to America and get back together with Michelle.

Soon after, Swami called the students to the Jesus Temple where he was sitting in his chair with a group of people. I sat in the corner near the bathroom. I was disgusted with everything and not very happy about the whole thing. I didn't know what was coming next.

He motioned for me to come up, but I wouldn't go. I was in such a bad mood that I didn't want to go near him. I just looked down and ignored him. He got up and came over, went to the bathroom, then came out and talked to me. I was sitting on the floor. He said a little bit, reassuring me. I don't remember exactly how he put it, something like, maybe right now you can't see it but something good is coming from all of this. There's a reason for all of this, you will see.

I was immersed in it then, so his words didn't make me feel much better. He knew I was in the trough and just couldn't see. The thing that was really sweet was his tone, and how he reassured me. His telling me that did help. Although I didn't feel better, I knew I would recover. I just couldn't see it at the time. Swami was compassionate and kind; he let me know that it would get better.

Years later, I learned why Swami acted this way. The karmic relationship between Michelle and I would have led to a different life altogether. I would have had to return to America to fulfill those responsibilities. The relationship karma had to be fulfilled either by living it through or following Swami's instructions. When a guru gives instructions and you follow them, the guru takes the karma rather than you. In my case, he paid the karma. Instead of years of living out a relationship that would pull me away from spirituality, I went his way, with some pain upfront but him taking the bulk of it. It takes faith and trust, but I can say now I am so grateful to him for saving me from that fate.

Interesting relationship leelas still continued over the years. I assume these were all karmic ties that needed to be undone. One evening, Swami called all the women in the ashram for a meeting with him. I heard the runners going around, notifying every room that Swami had called them to the Mandir.

I happened to be walking over to go on duty for the evening as the women were leaving from the meeting. There were quite a lot of women, most I didn't know. I was walking in the opposite direction and could see the women looking at me, and kind of intensely. I could feel their energy; it was weird. I was wondering, 'Do I have something on my shirt? What is it? Why are they looking at me?'

When I got on duty, I found out. In the meeting, Swami said there was going to be a new Mrs. Clark. The woman didn't know my last name so other people had to tell her it was me. Of course, everyone thought if Swami said it, it must be true. It was the first I was hearing about it.

I decided I should probably spend some time with her to see what Swami was up to. So, I talked to her a little when I had time around my duties. It became clear we were not a good fit for anything. After I spent more time with her, I started purposefully pinching her to cut the energy between us. I tried to show her I really didn't think that we would be very compatible. I said things I hoped would upset her. I did a bunch of things that I thought were kind of mean, not even one fazed her.

Soon after, Swami sent the students to *Hospet*. While in Hospet, we had a restriction that no woman could go into town on their own. Hospet is a crossroads town, so there is good shopping and a good selection of inexpensive saris. One of the big things the women wanted to do was go out shopping. They had to have a man with them, so I became an escort. One woman would sign up, I would go to town with her then come back and get the next one. Of course, some of them took way longer so I was running late. My "fiancé" was scheduled for later in the day and I was late. She had a fit. I was being disrespectful to her. She really let me have it. Everyone else was happy that I was willing to spend all day shopping at sari stores with them. Anyone who knows sari stores in India would agree it was commendable.

But she was so angry, she quit talking to me. And for that one, I didn't even try! It happened all on its own. It was an accident. I had pinched her harder than I did when I was trying. After that, she completely blew me off. I was extremely relieved.

Fortunately for me, Swami never brought it up again.

Another time, Swami told a student that she and I were going to get married. He didn't tell me. We went on a group trip to *Shirdi*, and I was told which vehicle to sit in. I wasn't in the vehicle with her. By the time we got to the restaurant, she was upset because she had expected me to sit with her. In her mind, I was her future spouse. I didn't know exactly what was going on, but I suspected Swami had been fueling this. I wasn't feeding it; I wasn't interested in her. She didn't know I was already in a relationship with someone else since it wasn't public. She projected her expectations and anger at me, based on what Swami had told her.

When we went to the restaurant, most everyone had been seated and a place had been saved for me next to Swami. I had to walk in front of everyone to sit down next to him. She got upset with me for not sitting next to her. It was an impossible situation. I couldn't tell her about my relationship because Swami had asked me to keep it private. I had to keep my word to him.

Swami put you in those kinds of situations, so you had to figure out how best to handle it. Maybe it was a test for me, or maybe he was just using me to work on her. He was always doing multiple things at once.

Swami on his northeast bed

Jesus Temple

Swami on his northeast bed

Swami in Jesus Temple

A New Phase Begins

My guru became my all-in-all, my home and property, mother and father, everything. All my senses left their places and concentrated themselves in my eyes, and my gaze was centered on him. My guru was the sole object of my meditation, and I was conscious of nothing else. While meditating on him, my mind and intellect were stunned, and I had to keep quiet and bow to him in silence.

-Sri Sai Satcharitra

After my promise to Swami, I saw and interacted with him daily. The more time I spent with him, the greater my appreciation for him grew. He was a spiritual person with a tremendous amount of energy and could do miracles. And yet, he had to do the daily stuff of a normal human. The staff needed to get paid, the bills needed to get paid, and he needed to meet with people often, sometimes all day. He had to do those things day after day.

While working in the office, we also started serving him as personal attendants. During the day, we would work in the office. In the evening, Swami would call and we would be on duty taking care of him.

I started with guarding the door of the living room at night when Swami was with students. Security at night, then helping in the office, then security in the morning. He specifically wanted me to be there in the mornings. Students would wait in the Jesus Temple and try to ask Swami questions when he had just woken up, before he even got to go to the bathroom! He didn't want people to still be there. He wanted me there in the morning to make sure no one was waiting outside his room.

He didn't explain things and would seldom have conversations with me. It was clear I was there to protect him from the students as well as the Indians. Especially the Indians at program times, I had to stand in the doorway and block them sometimes. It was a big adjustment for me to have to be aggressive to do my dharma.

After the Jesus Temple was built and was open, anybody could go up there whenever they wanted to. You could even sleep there at night. Swami was living on the ground floor in his apartment behind the Baba Temple at the time. His office was upstairs in the Jesus Temple. Often, he would work at night and invite people into the office.

I got to sit outside the door and watch people who came and went. I would hear the laughter inside the room, often roaring. Everyone was laughing and having a great time on the other side of the door. I would sit and try to stay awake. Occasionally, I would get invited in. This was something I figured Swami used to work on people's egos – who got picked to go into his living room at night. Usually, it wasn't me, but it didn't bother me. Guarding the door wasn't much of a job; it was just a bunch of students going in and out. It didn't seem like I did much, but he wanted me there, so I did it.

Soon Swami told me that my time for meditation was done, and from now on my path was purely *seva*. From then on, my full focus changed to serving Swami, and for the rest of Swami's life, I purely was a seva character.

Swami also told me he would intentionally create suffering for me because going through it would enable me to receive greater energy later. It was like I was building my bank account for the future. It's an advanced concept to understand. Swami would deliberately push me into uncomfortable situations and push me to the edge of my comfort zone, which I knew was in my best interest.

Some people ask why you need a guru. Well, I can say personally, I would never have gone as far on my own as he pushed me to go. I had been a spiritual student for many years before I met him. I had some capacity; I meditated a lot. But he would consistently push me beyond my capacity to increase it, way more than I could ever do on my own.

I knew that it was a huge gift that Swami allowed me to serve and be around him. But sometimes, it was grueling. At the end of his life, Swami could go three or four days without sleeping. The thing is, he would say goodnight and go to his bedroom, then it would take me about an hour or an hour and a half to clean up. When all the rooms were cleaned, I would go. I would lay down but would be up an hour later. If he slept for two hours, I got one hour. Then it would start again. It was an incredible opportunity to push me beyond my limits, beyond what I ever thought possible.

The Quiet Voice in My Mind

Swami didn't spend much time talking to me or teaching me things directly. That had started when I was doing sadhana under the tree. He would walk by me on his way to check on the Vaastu of the ashram while I was sitting doing japa. I would feel him inside, calling me. Then as I would look, he would be walking across the garden waving at me. He didn't stop, he just would go by. Sometimes he would just smile and continue along.

Swami would tell us we need to be in silence. He gave powerful mantras that brought people into thought-free trance states very easily. He wanted us to learn to bring that silence into everything we did in daily life. That was my main process.

Doing japa develops inner silence. You get your mind under control; you get it quiet. When you are quiet, you can hear the master. It just continued that way for me. This was my main sadhana. Sometimes, when I was on duty, I would just feel, 'I need to do this now.' Generally, it was correct. I would get a feeling that I needed to go to him, he needed water, whatever. It could be a simple thing. He sometimes would act surprised, like, 'Oh, I was going to call you and there you are!' I felt that was what I needed to continue to develop. Once you get a taste for that, you get an intuition and act on it and get a positive response, then you continue to listen to that.

Information comes only in the silence. I didn't know who was feeding that information to me, but it was consistent. I don't know if it was one of his angels, or directly from Swami. But I knew to hear it, I had to be still, and needed some meditation power.

You must be able to sit still and develop silence. That is where things begin. We can talk about esoteric things but if you can't sit still, you are not eligible. If you are consistent and work at it, you can do it, but it takes effort. I sat in the back and could tell who was present by their energy. Once you experience the silence, you can see it and feel it in those who have it.

I had some experience working with my mind studying with the Toltecs. It was a gift to meet Don Miguel earlier because I had real tools to quiet my mind. *The Four Agreements*[23] are simple, but that doesn't mean they are easy to do. I

---

[23] Toltec teachings by Don Miguel.

practiced those teachings and had huge results quieting my mind. I had used them long enough before I met Swami to know they worked. At first, it seems impossible because you think you are your mind, you think that is you. First is to realize you even have a choice when the mind tells you something. If you just react without thinking, doing what your mind is telling you, it escalates and gets worse. If you realize you have a choice, and your happiness depends on your choice, you can choose not to listen to the mind. Once you start disassociating yourself from your mind, you can start associating with that stillness. The more I did that, the more I was drawn to stillness. It becomes a self-perpetuating cycle. You need to be diligent; you need to pay attention, you need to know you have a choice, you need to choose silence over the mind and reactivity, then you can grow that silence. I probably had a little better control than most, and that control came from practice. The silence grew, and the contrast between the silence and my mind got bigger. At first the mind is completely in control, and you have very little stillness. Maybe in the evening before you go to bed, or on a train with a repetitive noise, you can experience stillness. But if you practice, you can really go.

The other Toltec teaching that held me in good stead was not to take anything personally. I had been practicing that, so when Swami would be upset and pinch me, I didn't take it personally. If I took it personally, I would crash. If I crashed, I wouldn't be doing any good for myself or for him.

In the beginning on duty, I spent a lot of time meditating in the Jesus Temple. When it was just me and Swami, it was often really quiet! That was a big part of my time with him. We would often just be together in the silence, while he was on his northeast bed. Hours and hours, not interacting, not talking, both meditating in the silence.

Other times he would be very active, so he would call groups and I would be there to serve them. It was kind of dreadful when he would call them because I liked it quiet. I think some students assumed it was going all the time. For me, it was the exception, mostly it was quiet. At least at the beginning.

Sometimes when I was on duty, I would finish everything that I had to do. All the rooms would be clean, and everything would be set and ready to go. I always had projects to work on, but most of them I couldn't do there. So, if I finished all my work, I would just sit down and meditate. I figured that was a good use of my time. Maybe it was my sense of duty, but I wouldn't leave. I didn't want anyone to be there when he got back, I wanted to make sure he had a safe environment. Whenever Swami happened to see me meditating, he always smiled. He really liked it when I meditated there. I was there for a reason. I took it seriously.

Swami always communicated with the softest, quietest voice in my mind. You could only hear it if your mind was quiet. If I was in a chaotic place personally, I would miss it. I always had to be careful with my energy. What was I doing, what was I thinking about, how did I feel in my body? If I was tense and upset, I would miss that quiet voice. Without silence, I couldn't hear him. So going on duty was always when I knew that it took quieting my mind.

The best compliment for me was being able to surprise him. It meant I was very quiet inside and outside. In this state, I could check on him, take care of him without disturbing him, especially when he was resting or meditating. I would switch the water bottle at the edge of his bed for a cool bottle. Then I would see him reach for water and could tell he was surprised it was cold. I had walked out to his bed and was able to exchange bottles without his notice.

When it was cold, we put hot water bottles under his covers so it would be warm when he laid down. The water bottle had to be changed every couple of hours whether he was there or not. In the summer, he had a water cooler by his bed. If he stayed on his bed for a long time, I would have to fill the cooler while it was running. It was right next to the head of his bed, and it had to be full. If he was there more than four hours, I had to sneak over and fill it. Everything I did for him was an exercise in learning how to not disturb him.

In the Jesus Temple, I would see something on the floor, a leaf or something, and think I should pick that up but would be too busy. Later, Swami would come in and tell me to pick up the leaf, and look at me like, 'I already told you!' That was the thing, he made it obvious; I needed to listen to that voice. I needed to be quiet enough, I needed to have my mind calm. You can never tell what mood an avadhut will be in. Some days, super quiet, nice. Other days, politicians, car accidents, police, anything could be running. Being a support for him I had to be quiet and calm. Even if things were very busy, full of activity, but inside, that calmness. Maybe it didn't happen all the time, but I had to try to always be listening. He responded to that, and it helped him.

Swami was not the voice screaming loudly in my mind. He was the one moving his eyes and expecting me to see what he was indicating. You can only see that if you are looking and are paying attention. If you are not paying attention, you won't see it. It's like Baba says, "Look to me, then I will look to you." Swami expected that.

To hear your intuition, the master's guidance, you have to be in silence. Your mind has to be quiet. Your mind is a bullhorn, but the master is standing behind you whispering. You have to learn to become quiet so you can hear that voice. Serving Swami forced me to learn to be quiet, both internally and externally. He liked when people around him were peaceful and walked gently without disturbing anyone. It demonstrated their inner silence and awareness. Everything I did for Swami was an exercise in learning how to not disturb him. Even though I tried my best, it wasn't always possible.

As a mechanic when I was young, there were certain problems I couldn't figure out. Often the answer would come when I was quiet. Not when I was working on it, thinking about it. In the evening, after work, I would get an intuition about what it would be, then I would try it. I can say that mostly the intuitions were right. You learn that when that intuition comes you need to pay attention to it. How do you strengthen that? By acting on it. Not just that you heard it, but if you act on it, then your intuition gets stronger, more consistent. You develop confidence in yourself. It's like a muscle, the more you exercise it the stronger it becomes. I had to stop thinking about it, stop hammering on it, just letting it go, and then it would come. If you exercise restraint of your mind by meditating or being in silence, that cycle quickens. With Swami, it was a quickening of something that already existed.

The other side was that every time I went against my intuition around him, I got in trouble. I could feel that I was doing something that was off. He never missed it if I went against my intuition. He always did something that made it apparent that I wasn't getting away with it. He was strengthening the ability to listen. He didn't have to say 'you could do better,' he just acted on it. As soon as it would happen, I would know it; I knew better. He was consistent with that. If I did something and had the intuition that I shouldn't be doing it, he confirmed it. Even with small things, like my clothes. If I wasn't comfortable with the clothes I had on, he would tell me to change them. There was nothing wrong with the clothes, except I didn't like them. It's a small thing except if I am going against myself, he would feel it and point it out.

Early on, another attendant asked Swami many personal questions about her life, and he seemed open to answering her. I always had the feeling that it would not be appropriate for me, but one time I asked one small thing. He didn't say anything, but gave me a scathing look. I had gone against myself, I asked him something I knew I shouldn't ask. He didn't make a big deal about it, but he did look at me to be sure I got the point.

To be around Swami meant learning to live in silence and be guided by intuition. Generally, I didn't take a shower or change my clothes until just before I went on duty to be sure they were clean. One day, I had just gotten up and walked in the ashram, wearing my clothes from the day before. Another attendant was going on duty, and I offered to carry one of the big bags she had. I followed her over to the Mandir. In general, I didn't want to be seen by Swami before duty time because he could call me and have me stay. So, of course, on that day he came out and immediately said, 'I was going to call you. You have to stay here, and she needs to leave.' You could say it was intuition.

The way I felt about it, I was drawn to go there. I can't say why I was in the right place and the right time and volunteered to help. It's that kind of thing, it isn't necessarily conscious. I just showed up at the right time. It can be that simple, just do what's in front of you. When you are silent you find yourself in the right place, not even thinking.

Of course, it doesn't mean that you are fully prepared! I was in last night's clothes and hadn't eaten. I told the attendant that I didn't have any clean clothes, she said, "You should just wear Swami's clothes!" I would never do that and was horrified she even suggested it.

I just washed my face and hands in the sink then prepared for some VIPs to arrive. I went over and sat where I could hear the cars coming without being seen and just waited. Of course, I got bored. I took out the fountain pen in my pocket and took the cap off and proceeded to drop it on my thigh! Green ink went through my white kurta, my pants, my underwear and onto my skin! Just then, the car with the VIPs drove up! There I was with green ink all over my clothes. I ran in the back and rinsed my kurta and realized there was no way it was coming out. Sure enough, I ran back to Swami's clothes. I knew which of Swami's clothes were his 'fat clothes' and picked out a kurta and pants. I took my clothes off, put his clothes on and was ready to go! His pants fit me, but his kurta top was a little tight but it worked, I was there the entire night on duty serving the VIPs.

Developing a Relationship with God

What has touched your heart to God is the seed of exiting the illusion. Develop those treasure moments, practice them, believe in them. Do it as a practice; it is a mechanism. Keep those tender-hearted feelings ever fresh, ever innocent, vulnerable. Vulnerable to surrender to another, vulnerable to worship God in another. If we want to truly worship, we must have that vulnerability. We must celebrate it. Not to the world but to God, to our hearts. That is mastery. To be in the presence of a master may look like different things, but it will feel the same. You will know it's real by your inner feelings. You will know, nobody will have to tell you.

-Nityanandaji

If you want a relationship with God, you have to think about God and do things that remind you of God. You have to keep God in your awareness. Spirituality is about developing awareness.

When Swami walked into the Jesus Temple, the first thing he would do is look at Jesus. I watched Swami do this consistently for years. He didn't stop, but every time he walked in, he looked. He always turned to look to God first. I don't know what he was doing when he looked, but he would always look. I had to train the students cleaning the altar not to put anything in the way or he could trip. I figured he was acknowledging, saying hello, giving thanks. Every time he walked in, he did that. I did that, too. I would walk in the Baba Mandir, look, put a sankalpam or give thanks. I do that in the Datta Temple here[24] as well, walk in the room, first thing, look and give thanks. It doesn't have to be a big deal. I don't have to walk up; I don't have to pranam. That's another way to do it. For me, I walk in and right away give thanks.

It makes it personal. It becomes more of a conscious relationship to God. If you practice it, you don't have to think about it. It becomes habit. It just takes a second to acknowledge and thank God first. Even if Swami was walking and talking on the phone, he would look. If he was in the middle of something, even then, he would look.

---

24 Divine Mother Center.

It doesn't take a huge production. That's the real thing, it's not going up in front of everyone and holding on for 20 minutes and telling your life story! Ninety percent of the time people are spaced out and babbling, not being focused. Instead, short and direct, then bing! Done.

Swami worked that way. When I was meditating under the tree, I could feel his sankalpam directed at me as he walked by. He looked at Jesus and bing, there it goes, he sent it. Today when I drive out of the Center,[25] I look at the Baba *murthi* on my way out and, bing, thank him or ask for protection. When I drive out, I look at him. Then he knows I am thinking of him. It isn't a big production, but I remember to do it every time with sincerity.

To say happy Guru Day[26] to Swami would make his day. But it would have to be heartful. Authentic, not rote. You just want to experience your relationship as a real thing, as a living give and take. Acknowledge that relationship. What else can you give to God? Your attention is a real thing. Of course, you must believe that it is God, that it's Baba there, not a statue. One time somebody took garbage through the Baba Temple. Swami was not happy. To him, Baba was a living presence.

In India, there are dikshas about using your right hand or foot when entering a sacred place, or when handing or receiving something. This has been a part of Vedic culture for yugas. The temples have raised thresholds, so you remember to enter with your right foot. It forces you to pay attention, reminding you it is a sacred space, enter with your right foot.

Swami was a stickler about it. You didn't walk into his office leading with your left foot and you didn't hand him anything with your left hand. Anything. He would refuse it. We threatened to tie one attendant's left hand behind his back! He just couldn't remember. He would use his left hand and Swami would refuse it or make him do it again. The attendant had to pick it up again with his right hand. Once in a great while if he was in a hurry, he would just hand me something and I would have to grab it with my left hand. But normally, no. It was developing awareness. In the Dwarkamai, he was even more strict. He told groups, "If any of your members step in with the left foot first, it will crash the process. The process is over." They had to post someone at the door to remind

---

[25] Divine Mother Center.
[26] Thursday.

people. The saints in India will always look to see if you entered a process leading with your left foot. If you did, you were automatically disqualified.

I had to learn how to notice the details in my environment. Every day I would walk to the Mandir to go on duty. Swami would ask me for details about things happening in the ashram, like the construction. He would get annoyed if I did not notice. He taught me to pay attention to my surroundings.

We have to develop awareness in every aspect of our lives. If you don't have awareness about simple things, how do you think you are going to have God-awareness? How do you think you are eligible for consideration by God?

If I am on the lookout for the big miracle, but trip over things because I am not paying attention, where's the clarity? As John Hiatt sang, "You wouldn't know a burning bush if it blew up in your face!" If you are not aware of where you are and what you are doing, yet expect a miracle, it doesn't make sense. You have to learn to pay attention to the basic things first. People who want the experience of a divine miracle like darshan are tripping over their shoes and certainly not recognizing the subtler things. You must have a level of silence and mindfulness before you can recognize.

Listen to Swami talk about *tricky darshans*. If you can't see something right in front of you in your everyday life, how do you expect to recognize a tricky darshan? Having awareness only when I am meditating but not in my day-to-day action, would not work at all with Swami.

Inner Attunement

The practical part of taking care of Swami was easier to explain than the energetic. The energetic part of interacting with him was harder. Everything went according to his energy. You could do the same thing two days in a row, and it would be a home run out of the ballpark, the next day it was totally inappropriate, and that just depended on his energy. To have a sensitivity to interact with him in a way that didn't disturb him – that was an art. That required an internal connection, sensing his energy and being in tune with that. That is such a big part of the master-student relationship, the attunement with the master. That was the most important part of my work with him, and key to understanding how to interact with the avadhut energy.

Swami never talked to me about what he was doing, with his own process or with students or anything else. He didn't tell me where he was going, it was up to me to know the sounds of the ashram and figure out where he was and when he would need me. There was a rhythm to the ashram. In the evenings there would be *bhajans*, and then *Aarthi*. When I was upstairs on duty Swami would never say, "I'm going downstairs to give a talk." I would be cleaning the bathroom and notice the singing had stopped which meant he was there. I would run downstairs. I had to pay attention every minute to what was going on around me, as well as listening internally. I needed to be attuned to him through my consciousness.

One day, there were two new attendants. They were asking me questions because they were nervous about interacting with Swami. At that moment, Swami opened the door, came part way down to the landing, and asked for something. The new attendants didn't understand a word he said. So I repeated back to Swami what he asked for. The attendants just looked at me, 'How did you do that?' It took years of training and having an ear for what is being asked. I hadn't realized how much training I had had until I saw someone new struggling. As much as understanding his actual words, it was the attunement to him to being able to understand him and what he needed.

Part of this attunement was an inner state of mind, and part of it was simply paying attention to him. One of the funniest things for me was the time I learned how much I relied on being able to look at him to know what he needed. There was a time when my glasses were getting repaired, so I only had sunglasses. Swami would say something but without my glasses, I couldn't understand him! I had to walk close to him to understand him. I realized how much information I got from him visually, very little of it was hearing him, purely when looking at him I would understand what he wanted. Without my glasses, I had to get within about ten feet of him, which he wasn't used to. He got super irritated at me!

When I was on duty, I sat on the floor near the doorway of the Jesus Temple while Swami would be in his northeast bed. He would be laying out there and make a gesture with his hand, which meant that he wanted incense. He wouldn't say anything, he would expect me to be sitting there watching him and noticing his hand. He had another motion for turning the sound up. He would be laying on his bed making these simple hand gestures and expecting me to see it and to do what he asked. He preferred not to have to say anything. I could feel him get annoyed if he had to tell me what he wanted. He wanted me to know what he wanted. His attitude towards me was, 'You are going to make me say it?' That was repeated numerous times, by the time he had to say it, it was too late. The higher the energy went, the more he expected you to just know, so he could look at you and you would do it. But what does that take? You have to pay attention and be quiet. It was always about just watching him, even if I didn't understand what he was doing, just be watching. Try to be one step ahead of him.

Often in my interactions with him, he wouldn't say if I was doing something incorrectly, I would just feel it. He would make a face or give a look, and I would know. So, part of the attunement was being sensitive to the subtle feedback he was giving me.

Learning to be around Swami was about how to be with Mother Divine. It was completely unpredictable; you never know what will happen. You had to follow the energy. There were certain things to do to handle that energy. The most important thing was that softness, that open heart, that sensitivity to him. I would get a feeling of when I could get away with things and when I couldn't. You could ask him things when he was open. In a short interaction, you could tell right away if it was the right time or not, and if it was the wrong time, you could not back out fast enough! But if it was the right time, he was receptive. There would be times I had 20 questions and he would answer every single one and ask for more. But you could never corner him. Any time you wanted to interact and ask him questions, it always had to be up to him. He was the lead. You could never push him to decide. It would not end well if you tried to command on him; his consciousness was the consciousness in charge. It was really a training to always surrender to that.

My Path Is Now Seva

I went to India as a student. In those early years, Swami gave a lot of healing techniques, and taught a lot of information. I was learning that knowledge and made recordings and listened to them like he asked us to. A year or so into my time there, he told me my time for meditation was done, it was time for seva. I was still really interested in being a student. I wanted to help the world; I wanted to help people.

For a while he left me a little bit in between. When I first started doing seva for him I was still participating in some of the student programs. If there was a program, typically everyone would attend. For a short time, I wasn't sure if I should try to go, but then he directly said to me, "You are seva only, guru seva." I was no longer a student. I was no longer included.

There were times when I went to a talk, and he would look at me and say, "Why are you here?" I was like, "I am trying to participate!" Then he would kick me out. It became clear, this is my path, to take care of him. Did it matter that I still wanted to be a student? My feeling was this is what he chose for me. At least I knew about *Venkusa* and Baba. Nityanandaji told me about that, he helped me to see early on that this was a viable path. But it was not what I imagined when I came to India. I was familiar with being a student, with learning knowledge. One part, I really liked it. I gave that up without an understanding of how it would look or what it would be like.

When I began my seva for him, I was still trying to do the moon meditations, to hold onto some practices. It wasn't long before I just couldn't do that. I asked Swami about it; I was getting overcooked by trying to do everything. His answer was ambiguous; he didn't say don't do it, but I would be on duty with him, so it was physically impossible. Or if I had been on duty all night, I was just too tired to do it. It became clear that I could not take care of him and keep up with practices.

There were times where everyone in the ashram had to stay in their rooms. It could be because VIPs were visiting, or other saints, and he didn't want Westerners out and around. You would get a message for that. My feeling was yahoo! I get a night off, then the message would come – not you! I would have to go on duty. Maybe it wasn't such a big deal, but it took me some time to get comfortable feeling like I was missing something.

Doing japa sitting under the tree was more my idea of what enlightenment would look like. Instead, I got the chaos of running behind Swami, cleaning his bathroom, getting him food and water, and dealing with students' craziness. Sometimes I wished I could be out under the tree enjoying that peacefulness! Sometimes other students would complain about their japa, and I would think, 'Oooh, I would love to have hours of japa to do!!'

126

But I knew Swami was taking care of me. He had me join in different group processes at the end of their process to receive the energy. I would not know anything about what they were doing or the aim of their process. Often, they would be chanting a mantra I didn't know. Sometimes Swami would say, "I am going downstairs to check on something. You should come." Then when we got there, "Take your shirt off, sit down and meditate."

It was always a little strange for me to jump in at the end of a process. I had no guidelines, no diksha, no idea what they were doing. But I knew this was Swami's way of taking care of me. In all these processes, you receive various energies and blessings. He made sure I received them even though I hadn't done the sadhana because I was doing seva for him.

Swami would often stop me before my japa program had been completed. You can feel it when the japa starts running in you, you can feel the flow. Often, that is when he would stop me. I assumed that it was done. I had received the quantum of energy from the practice. That's the great value in having a guru, he can see what you are doing.

Mostly for me, he would never tell me that I was done with what I was doing, he would just give me something else to do. That's how I knew it was done. But whatever it was, I knew he was always taking care of me.

Truthfully, I had never wanted to serve Swami because I had seen the students close to my first guru. There was backbiting and fighting for a position to be physically close to the guru. I think that runs around every guru. I never wanted any part of it. I wanted to be out under the tree enjoying the energy. I didn't want to be dealing with a bunch of crazy people vying for position and power.

Over the years, Swami protected me from the jealousy of the students because they didn't see me as a threat, so it was a protection. I was never anybody important. He saved me. He also did things publicly that could lead other students to see me in a negative light. I think that was intentional.

Even so, some of the other students did end up being jealous. But the truth was, I knew how to talk to Swami in a way that didn't offend him. They didn't. Specific ways they interacted with him I had told them would not go well. They did it anyway.

Swami in front of Jesus

Sensitivity to the Master

The soul is very, very, very sensitive to whether there is love and devotion. The soul is cosmic energy – a piece of God. We must take care of it. The only way to approach the soul is to be relaxed, very polite, and very obedient. You must take care to be very sensitive. You cannot just issue a command for the soul to rise up. Only if you are sensitive, will your light grow.

-Sri Kaleshwar

Swami was extremely sensitive to energy. He was extremely particular about maintaining his vibrations and the vibrations of the environment wherever he was. He taught how important it is to maintain our vibrations and always be living in the positive. For him, everything had to be orderly and in its place. His space had to be sparkling and fragrant. The altars always tended and lights burning. It had to be maintained as a sacred place.

Part of the sensitivity needed was to never engage him before he was ready. This was especially true if it was negative news, or I needed something from him. It was his energy that was leading, not mine. I had to surrender to his energy. If I started to pull on him before he was awake or ready, it wouldn't end well. For me, one of the biggest things was to try and maintain a positive environment and take care of the simple things so he didn't have to think about it. And, most importantly, to be sensitive and attuned to his energy and the situations surrounding him.

Swami was peculiar about some of his personal things and habits. Sometimes we could understand why, but mostly not. It was part of the fragrance of his life. In the mornings, he needed time to reintegrate back into his body. Typically, he would come out of his bedroom and walk through the Jesus Temple to the bathroom. When he would come out, he would usually go to see Jesus. It was best to give him space, not bother him, or ask for things until he indicated he was ready. Generally, after he had been to Jesus, he was ready to engage. I would watch him through my peripheral vision. Usually, he would smile or let me know. I always waited to let him initiate when it was time to interact. I wouldn't look at him until he let me know he was ready.

Swami came to America to fish for souls. He was looking for students he had known from other lifetimes. He was looking for certain things. Of course, I don't know what he was looking for. I had a conversation with another senior student who had some background in Vedic knowledge. With him, the hook seemed to be knowledge-based. For me, I believe it was my sensitivity. I feel Swami was looking for someone who had sensitivity, and then developed that more in me.

Early on, Swami was doing a special teaching in the Baba Mandir. He asked for all the windows to be closed. One student jumped up and started slamming the windows shut, one after another. Every time, Swami jumped, I jumped. The student did not notice and just kept on running around like an elephant in the temple. There were people sitting in the room, no one else seemed to notice how Swami was reacting. He looked and saw that I noticed how it had affected him.

Swami was sensitive to noise. When Swami was living downstairs, Westerners were staying upstairs. People would walk heavily, making a lot of noise. It didn't matter how much people weighed; it was how they walked. If they weren't paying attention, they would stomp, which was loud downstairs. Swami made comments in public about it, "They are pounding on my head!" He looked right at me when he said it. It disturbed him. At first, I thought, 'Is he saying that I am walking like that?' But I realized he was acknowledging that he knew it was also disturbing me!

Swami was extremely sensitive to his environment in all ways, including temperature. If he would go into the office and was warm, he would turn the AC to the coldest setting. He was fine when he was in the room, but if he would leave and come back and there was too big a difference, he would comment. You just had to pay attention to him. If he got up and left, you had to raise the temperature on the AC so it would be cool but not a big contrast. The same with his bed in the winter and in summer. The cooler had to be filled and ready. In winter, the hot water bottle had to be in his bed, so it wasn't cold when he got in. Having a hot water bottle in his bed meant he was warm when he got under the covers, he liked that. I was always paying attention to those kinds of things to take care of him.

Swami was extremely attuned to my movements. I noticed that if I did anything, he would look at me. He told me he was particularly attuned to me at public programs. That meant I had to be careful about my movements. Any physical moves I made would pull his attention. I had to learn to be still. Extremely still. Partially that's why I sat in the back. I knew that if I fidgeted, he would look. I was there to serve him, not to pull on him or distract him. Purely, I was his support. I didn't approach him or talk to him. If he was outside meeting with people, he didn't want me to be seen. If he saw me, he would assume I wanted something so he would call me over. It would irritate him if I didn't need anything.

One day, I saw Swami laying on his northeast bed with a peacock right near him. I knew it would disturb him. I thought if that thing screeches, it's going to wake him up! I walked over and kind of waved my arms to get the peacock to fly off without bothering Swami. I couldn't do much. I got right by Swami's bed and was flailing my arms when the peacock screeched and woke him up. The peacock was at the foot of his bed and let out the biggest screech possible. Swami woke up and saw me flapping my arms just a couple of feet away! I thought it couldn't get any worse. Swami didn't say anything, but later he shared with a group of us that he had been up all night doing japa and had just gone to sleep when the peacock came and woke him up. He was illustrating how the illusion can hit you.

If Swami was in his swing, he knew if I was hanging around the front of the Mandir, I wanted something. There was a reason. Times like that, it was important that my physical presence was there, but I was not thinking, 'Swami, I need to ask this question.' All that would do was pull on him and disturb him. If I needed to ask him a question or have some interaction with him, my physical presence was enough. I had to stay calm and maintain my clarity. Mostly if he was outside, I would stand around the corner where he couldn't see me. In a public talk, that was different, then I would sit on the staircase in the back. I liked to sit in the back so he knew where I was.

Generally, if he was outside, the Indian staff would take care of him. My area was upstairs and private. But sometimes the staff needed help so I would hang around to support them. But I would not let him see me. I could be around and help them if they needed something.

Sometimes Western students would see me waiting and think I was just standing around. They would think I wasn't doing anything when the reality was, I had to stay alert to be ready to talk to him. Sometimes I would be in the attendant's room and look out the window to see if he was in his swing. It was a way I could be invisible. When he was in between things, I could run out and see if I could approach him. I knew he could feel that I had a question no matter how careful I was with my energy, but I wanted to minimize my pulling on him. Because of his sensitivity, even me just thinking about him could be a disturbance.

I discovered just how disturbing it was to have people thinking of me and wanting something from me. Once, I told a student that I had a water filter that he could use to make water for his family. I told him it would work best for me if he could fill up a couple of cases at a time so I wouldn't be disturbed. But he did exactly what I didn't want. He was always trying to find me so he could get water. I was just way too busy for that. But the real problem was, I could feel him thinking about me. He would pull on me by thinking about me and needing something from me. I was trying to help him, but it turned into a big pain.

Swami said he had thousands of people thinking about him. I just had one and that was terrible. I made some comment to Swami about how disturbing it was, and the next day it was gone. It wasn't the only time that happened. I believe it was a boon I had that when I told Swami about something like that, he would just cut it off and it would stop. Saints deal with this all the time. It was not fun, most of the energy directed at them is pulling and blaming. People always want something from them or blame them. That's why they are called saints!

Swami told me not to let people touch me. Because I was close to him, he expected me to act appropriately in public. In general, I would not stand close to women, I would not smile too much. I was being judged by the Indian staff by Indian standards, even though I was a Westerner. I had to be careful about who I talked to. The Western thing is if you haven't seen someone in a while, they would hug you. There were a few awkward moments that I would step away from someone who would go to hug me. Even if it was in front of everyone, I would have to say it's better if you don't touch me.

Swami had said that if people touch him, he will feel their energy for three or four days. What would happen for me is if people touched me, they would come into my thoughts. When I was quiet, they would be circling. I would think about them, they would intrude on my silence. It became important to me to minimize who I touched. So, it was a social etiquette thing that he had me do, but it was also a protection. I am still sensitive to touching people.

Swami complained in public about me being too sensitive. What I believe was it was one of the main things that allowed me to take care of him. He said he was going to make me tougher. In fact, he made me more sensitive. I went completely the opposite direction from what he said!

Swami giving shaktipat initiation, 2010

Taking Care of Him

The people serving him couldn't see who Swami was. Serving him was a huge boon; if you could really see him, you wouldn't be able to function. That meant some people closest to him couldn't see his greatness. They could only see part of it. It made sense not to let me ask questions. He did that to keep me from understanding what he was doing.

My role was to support him, keep him comfortable, make sure he ate, the mundane things, but they had to be done. To do those things, he had to make sure I didn't get lost in the bigger picture.

The simplest part of taking care of Swami was the physical aspect. Every morning before Swami came out from his bedroom, students cleaned the large altar where there were murthis of Jesus, Mary, and Dattatreya. Fragrant jasmine garlands and burning oil lamps were maintained meticulously.

There were pictures and small murthis of deities and saints in all the areas that Swami lived. All of them had to have fresh jasmine garlands hung on them. Every morning and evening, we would hang the garlands around all the photos in his office, living room, and theater room. It took 30 to 40 minutes to put the flowers up. We cleaned the floor with rose water. When you entered his room, it was sparkling and fragrant. After finishing, people said they could smell us coming!

Once he came out of his bedroom in the morning, he would walk through the Jesus Temple, and go into his bathroom. Then I would immediately go into his bedroom, make his bed, and tidy up his room before he came out. Everything had to be done like he was never there.

He would come out of the bathroom and immediately go to Jesus. Then I would go into his bathroom. It was the same thing with the bathroom: clean the floor, pick up his clothes, go through his pockets (he always left something in there), clothes in the laundry, clean the shampoo off the walls.

If he was going to leave the temple right away, I would have some minor interaction with him. He would choose the scarf that he was going to wear. As I stood by the door, I would look at him and make sure that he was dressed nicely, his hair combed, and everything was in place. Generally, Swami was super good at that, but I was there to support him. If he chose a scarf with some loose threads on it, I always had a pocketknife and would take it out. I would never touch him without permission, but I would tell him, "Swami, there's a loose thread. Can I cut it off?" He would let me, and off he would go.

Sometimes he would sleep on his northeast bed, and it was the same process. After he got up and went to the bathroom, it was all cleaned when he got back, and a new water bottle replaced the old. It was different in the evening. Generally, Swami would be in the living room or office. Before I left for the night, I would always clean up the office, so it was ready in case he got up after I left. It was typical for him to do that. He would dismiss me, then the next morning, I would come and find plates on the table and see he had eaten.

For a while, the attendants were there for fixed times. When the next shift came, I would never say goodbye to Swami. The next attendant came, and I ran out of there. One thing, it could be pulling on him if I stuck around. The other thing was, he could give me another assignment before I left! I figured if he wanted me back, he would just call me. This happened a lot, especially when meeting with certain groups, he never hesitated to call me back.

Before I went to India, I did construction work. I would wake up with the sun and would often go to sleep before dark. Swami's mode was purely at night. He often stayed up all night. It was a big change for me to go from being a day person to being a night person.

When I went on duty, I had no idea what would happen or if I would be there for hours or days. Students would be going to early morning abhishek, often I was just getting off duty. That is when I would go back to my room to sleep. I would sleep as much as I could during the day to be ready to be on duty the next night. Sometimes, it would be eight hours. Sometimes, four. Sometimes, none. Sometimes he would ask me not to leave the temple and sleep in his apartment above the Jesus Temple. No change of clothes. Not anything. I would just stay there with him and not go home. I have never slept very well there. Sometimes he would let me send somebody to the apartment to bring me a fresh set of clothes, sometimes not.

It was a different perspective each day, and I had no idea how long I would be gone. 'Okay, whatever it is.' You have to surrender. It is austerity.

A Fun-loving Guy

The majority of Swami's life with his students, the way of his behavior, the way of his talking, is comedy, and at the same time, his actions are very straight. But majority, I'm really a big comedian. I like to laugh, and I make everybody laugh, especially when I'm relaxing. Once I pick up the jokes, period, it's a bliss. That's the bliss. That is prema (love) there. That is shanti (peace) there. That is dharma (right action) there. That is satya (truth) there too.

-Sri Kaleshwar

Swami had a great sense of humor. He loved to fool around, tease, and laugh with people. He was a sweet, fun-loving guy! He loved nothing more than jokes and laughter, and when we were all gathered around together, making everyone feel like they were one family. One of the ways he showed love was by teasing us. He loved to pretend to be different students and walk around like he was them! Pretending to be his students, he knew all our mannerisms, and how each person would act.

Once, he told me a story about himself. It was when he was living downstairs. Chitty, one of the Indian staff, was taking care of him as an attendant. He was managing Swami's living space and cleaning the bathroom. Swami told me when he was in the shower, he would soap up his hair and make his hair all funny and have conversations with himself. When he came out Chitty said, "Who are you talking to in there?" Chitty was very serious. Swami just laughed, he knew he couldn't tell Chitty he was just being silly and having fun in the shower. When Swami told it, he was really laughing and said, "Some of my staff think I am a little weird!"

A few times, I dropped things in the Jesus Temple, which broke on the marble. Or, sometimes when turning on a light, a light bulb would blow up and the glass would go all over the floor, which happens a lot in India. If Swami came out, I would tell him right away that a lightbulb blew up, "Swami, it's on the floor, be careful!" But Swami would just walk across, and his feet wouldn't get cut by the glass! You would watch him and hear him, *ch ch ch*. He just walked right over it!

Another time I was filling the refrigerator and dropped a glass bottle of Sprite. It was warm; it blew up and shattered into tiny pieces all over the temple floor. There was glass everywhere, and it was sticky. He was in the bathroom, so I knew he would come out and would have to walk by. It must have been 100 degrees and I was sweating like crazy trying to clean the floor. It was such a mess. Sure enough, he came out. I told him what had happened, but, same thing, not a peep. It didn't bother him at all. He just walked right over it, *ch ch ch*.

When we were in America, we were staying in L.A. In California, there are two area codes that have the same numbers but in a different order. I was in charge of putting the numbers in Swami's phones and had reversed the area codes. Swami called a number at two in the morning and got someone else. It turned out to be a woman who he talked to for 20 minutes! He said it was a nice conversation, but she wasn't who he wanted to talk to. He was only mildly irritated with me for getting the number wrong. I guess he had a nice conversation.

One afternoon, I was upstairs doing some maintenance in the Jesus Temple. I was on a ladder changing light bulbs and was wearing a kurta with the phone in my pocket. The phone rang just as Swami was walking by. I was holding a light fixture and couldn't let go of it. It was exactly the wrong moment to have my phone ring and was just the moment Swami happened to be walking by. He reached in my pocket, took the phone out, held it up, and told me to say hello. He listened to what the person said, then he gave the phone to me and told me what to say. This went on for a while. It turned out the person on the other end was Mataji! I had no idea who it was; he was too quick. Finally, she figured it out, and Swami started laughing! If you left your phone, anything could happen. If you were around Swami, you better have your phone on silent; he didn't want phones ringing. But if it did, he might just answer it. He could say anything. He also liked to call people, disguising his voice, which he was good at. He would say the funniest things to them! They would think it was a crank call.

Then there was the time that Swami wanted a two-line landline. Although it was common in America, I had the hardest time finding one in India. It was a huge headache to find that phone. When I finally got it, he made a big deal about it being a huge rush to get it working for him. When I got it installed and running, the first thing he did was call two women who really liked him but didn't like each other. He called each of them on one of his lines and had them talk to each other and made them think they were talking to him. He laughed and laughed, he had so much fun having those two women talk to each other. He had a lot fun playing with that phone.

Once, we were at the airport in Bangalore and there was a woman crocheting at our gate. He said, "She's knitting. I am going to go talk to her." I said, "Swami, she's not knitting; she's crocheting." He looked at me like, what do you know? He went over and she had no interest in talking to him! He came back right away and said, "You were right. I said she was knitting, and she got angry!" Of course, that didn't stop him. He went back to her and soon she was laughing!

When the Dwarkamai was first completed, he had a small group of men sleeping in there to do a meditation process. There was a very strict diksha about what we could bring in with us. We were only allowed to bring two towels, no clothes, no pillow, no metal jewelry, and nothing else. It was winter and it was cold.

After a few months, a group of women was brought in. I was sitting in the back while Swami was talking. Somebody knocked on the door, so I got up to answer it and my towel started to fall off! Luckily, I had noticed it was a little loose and grabbed it just before it fell down. Swami made a big joking deal about it. I said, "Everything was fine until you brought the women in here!" He got the joke and laughed! He teased me about getting darshan of my backside for some time afterward.

Swami would call Chitty in the middle of the night, and the first thing he would say was, "Oh, am I disturbing?" Chitty would always say no, but of course Swami was disturbing him! He was calling in the middle of the night! Swami always found that funny.

One time, a deer with a broken leg showed up at the ashram. They put a splint on it and the leg was healing. It was just a fawn when it arrived. After some time, its leg healed, and it was getting bigger. It had developed horns. It liked to follow Mr. Mani, the ashram manager, around. Mr. Mani oversaw the buildings at the ashram.

One day Mr. Mani was overseeing work in the gardens, standing with his legs spread and his arms across his chest. Suddenly, the little buck ran up from behind and wacked him in the groin with his horns! Swami was watching the whole scene from the verandah of the Jesus Temple. He laughed so hard. Then later when he told us the story, he had tears of laughter. He could hardly finish it. He thought it was the funniest thing. He had to put a towel over his head to stop laughing!

Normally, I always stayed in the background around Swami, but one time he wanted me to walk next to him. It was one of the few times I walked with Swami in public. We walked out through the main gate to a big event while I walked next to him down the road past the fountain. Hundreds of people were waiting as we walked by. While we were walking, Swami leaned over to say something to me, it looked like he was telling me something important. What he actually said was that I never missed an opportunity to sharpen my knife! He had a really funny look on his face. Then I realized what he was implying! He was just having fun.

Talking to Swami

Communicating

Swami never called unless he needed something. When he would call, he would do the Indian thing of being courteous and asking me questions. I would cut him off and say, "Why did you call, Swami?" It didn't annoy me, but I knew there was a reason he called, and he was beating around the bush. He could be pleasant, and it would be nice, but I always knew he didn't call to chit-chat. Swami didn't chit-chat with me. If he called, he wanted something. The sooner I got that, the sooner I could take care of it. I wouldn't be rude but would try to get him to tell me what he wanted so I could just take care.

Swami always wanted me to keep in touch. Anytime I would go to Bangalore, he wanted to know when I was leaving, I had to send him text updates with each thing I did. He wanted to know exactly where I was all the time. He kept me on a short leash. Even when I was in Bangalore, if I saw people there, I would say hello but couldn't stop and chat. Even if I was there for reasons other than errands for him, he expected me to keep in touch. I would have to send him text messages where I was and how long I would be gone.

On visa jumps it was the same way, I had to check-in, a minimum was to send a text when I left. He wanted to know where I was. If I went out of the country, he wanted to make sure I made it out and back safely.

One time I traveled to Sri Lanka on a visa jump with a German friend. She wanted to go exploring but Swami had told me not to go anywhere. That was fine with me, I was exhausted and happy to just relax in the hotel. I was in a hotel with no TV, no phones, no AC. It was quiet. It was heaven. Because there was no AC, it had slats with screens so I could hear the ocean when I went to bed and woke up. We would meet up and go out together for dinner once a day.

Swami had told me I should stay near the airport in case anything happened so I could get out of Sri Lanka. Ngumbo was the closest town to the airport with a beach, so we had compromised and stayed there. We went swimming in the afternoon before we left. We went to Bangalore, did some shopping, and traveled back to the ashram. It was a full day of travel.

She asked me if I would have to go on duty. I told her, you can never tell, but most likely. In Germany, she was a doctor that would go to crash scenes; she was used to an intense schedule. She was surprised that I might have to go on duty after a long travel day.

Sure enough, the taxi pulled up in front of the apartment building. I stepped out of the car, and Swami was on the roof. He called me on duty the minute I stepped foot out of the car! I went to my room, showered, changed clothes, and started on duty.

If you were on Swami's radar, you were on his radar.

Getting Instructions

When he gave me instructions, he could be funny in that he would give one instruction, then when he thought about it, add a second one. As he thought about it more, he would add a third one. By then, if you didn't have your notepad to write it down, you were in trouble. He could add a fifth, sixth, and seventh; then you were hurting! One way to help with that was to repeat back the instruction to him. Even then, you could repeat all seven, and then he would change it again because he had a chance to refine it. I could get four or five; then he would change. I always had a little pocket notepad and pen. Even if he gave only two instructions, I would repeat them back to him as soon as I understood. Then he would either acknowledge or change it. Then I would repeat it. I needed clarity. If I didn't have my notepad, I would write it down the first chance I got.

It would happen that someone would call with an important question for him that had to be asked immediately. If I turned around to him with that question, all those seven items he just gave me would disappear right out of my head. Then I would have to ask him for those items again, which was always a bad idea. You did not want to have to ask him anything twice.

Swami often asked me to do things that contradicted instructions he had already given to people. People would look at me strangely when I asked them things, and I had no idea what he had told them. I didn't care. I just had to do what he asked of me.

I tried to be careful not to hurt anyone's feelings, they were doing their seva, doing what they thought they should be doing. Generally, Swami was pushing me to hurry up the task and get it done. I had asked Swami if I could call him if there was a problem with any person. He said yes, but usually I didn't have to call. I only used that tact if I was desperate. If someone wouldn't listen, my trump card was, 'Let me call Swami and ask him,' or 'I'll call him, and you can ask him.' It always worked!

Sometimes Swami asked me to do things but didn't want me to say it was for him. I had to get people to do it without saying directly that it was a request from him. Mostly with the Indians, it wasn't a problem; they would just do it if I asked. The Indian staff knew I worked closely with Swami and were generally more respectful. Sometimes I felt that it was a test to see if I would get intoxicated with power. I never felt that I did, but sometimes people would really jump to help when I said stuff. But I always tried to be courteous to everyone.

Asking Questions

One of my jobs was asking Swami the questions students submitted to him. There was a constant stream that came in. Asking the students' questions was training for my own clarity. Especially in the beginning, he expected me to read the correspondence, highlight what I thought was most important, then ask him. I would give the student his reply. Sometimes we would read stuff and we would have it highlighted or underlined. Sometimes he would ask for a letter and I would just give it to him.

It took a lot of preparation; you had to have clarity with every question you wanted to ask him, and you had to be able to write the answers down as he was telling you, or as soon as he was done. If it was more than two or three questions, I would have to write them as he was giving them. I can't write fast; I would try to write the gist of it then fill the rest in later. I would write out what he said as close to word for word that I could remember.

Often, I would try to catch Swami by standing at the top of the staircase when he was going out. Usually, I would have a little black notebook. I would ask him if it was a good time to answer questions. If he said no, that was it.

Sometimes he would say later, sometimes he wouldn't say anything and just walk by!

He didn't have to say anything. If he didn't respond, it wasn't the right time. Sometimes he would say, "I need to go." Sometimes he was deep in thought and asking was an annoyance. He knew I was there and if I had something in my hand, I was going to ask him something. I had to learn how to be confident enough to ask Swami for his time but to accept if he wasn't interested and knowing that line between not getting any answers and annoying him. Rarely, he would stop and answer every single question I had.

Eventually, he stopped letting me ask him any student questions. My feeling was I was too good at it, and he would feel a little pinched or pursued by me. He just told me, "No more questions for you." I was so happy not have to do that since I always felt I was bothering him.

Swami would pinch me if I asked him a question and didn't have clarity. It forced me to tell students that they needed clarity before coming to him. It was hard to see the students' questions; they were long, they hadn't taken time to formulate or reflect on their questions.

I would say, "Ask your most important question first. What you interrupt his life for has to be worthwhile. Your first question has to interest him. The other thing is to have your questions written down, short and to the point. When you see him, you'll most likely forget everything. If he wants to, he can make your mind go blank. You'll have a really good time, really enjoy it, but he wouldn't have answered any of your questions." I tried to help people understand how to ask questions of Swami to get good answers. You could get an answer from Swami but if you didn't have clarity, it would not be a clear one. Often it didn't matter what I said. Invariably they would try to fix it by giving me the list of questions after they had met with him. I had to say, "No, sorry, you had your chance."

Swami told me that you can ask in one or two lines, that's it. That's plenty if you have clarity. If you are not clear, he will just reflect that to you, and you will come away with ten more questions. Some people didn't have any trouble, but many did. They would give me a letter to Swami with a question that was pages long. I would give it back to them. I would not tell them directly, you don't have clarity, but I would say, Swami doesn't speak English as his first language, you need to simplify this. I would get it back and it would be down to half a page, then I would hand it back and say try again until they got it down to one line!

Most people didn't know how to ask Swami questions in a way that they got helpful answers. Swami felt you should be able to distill any question down to one sentence. Some people gave questions like a flow chart. If they wrote it like that and expected him to answer yes or no, he would jump out and give an answer that was useless. They missed the mark right off the bat and he would go in a completely unexpected direction.

People wanted to impress Swami with their questions. But the way to impress him was to ask a concise question. Show that you understand by asking the right question. Your question reflects your consciousness. Some people would write a five-page letter that he didn't have tolerance for. I was appalled by the lack of clarity in their questions. It would kill my inspiration, and certainly did his.

Another mistake people made was thinking they had a better idea than Swami. Even if you thought you had a better idea than him, it was better to just do what he said, unless he asked. Just like Swami's experience with Baba, Baba would give him something he thought he could do in five minutes, and then Baba would make him go around this whole circuit to get back to where he would have been. But because he did that, things worked out way better than anything you could imagine. With Swami, it was that same way if he asked you to do something.

The other side of asking Swami a question if it was personal, if he gave you advice, you had to do what he said. Personally, I would much rather figure it out myself and only go to him about big things after I tried and was stuck. Students would come to Swami and ask him if they should do A or B. Typically, he would say Z. I would say, you asked the avadhut, now you need to do Z. People didn't like that! I had seen that enough to develop an attitude about being careful about what I asked. If you asked a question expecting a certain answer, it was pretty much a guarantee you would not get what you wanted.

As Westerners we are polite, we start with chit chat or small things, and save our big questions for last. Indians are different. You had to hook Swami with a good question right off the bat. It was better to do that than to chit chat or be polite, or ask simpler things first and work up to the most important.

With Swami, it was the reverse. You had to hook him, engage, and interest him, then after you did that, you could ask him anything.

Swami would interact with people differently; with some he had more willingness to answer basic questions. If you were around longer and your soul capacity was higher, he would hold you to a much higher standard. He would always answer process questions, personal questions not so much. With some group process questions, he would answer, but if they were trying to have a diksha adjusted, it was a compromise in the process. He would often accommodate them but still the first answer he gave was the best.

Mostly I didn't ask Swami personal questions. From the beginning, I did not want to pull on his time and attention. If I had a question I would hold it, see if it was valid, then do my best to figure it out. Often, Swami would answer my questions in public without my asking. That started early and continued all along. It showed me he knew where I was, I didn't have to verbally ask him. I received answers non-verbally, intuitively. That only works if you have silence.

I had witnessed Swami do Khandana Yoga, that was enough. If he was who I believed he was, I didn't need to ask him a lot. Things will become evident. Like I said about Mother Divine, She knows you better than you know yourself. What makes you think you need to tell Her what you need? For the most part, he would not answer my questions anyway. If I asked him something personal, he would just say figure it out. It meant that he had faith in me, faith that I could figure it out. Sometimes I wondered why he answered everyone else's questions but not mine. Everything I did with him was experiential, and if I didn't figure it out, he would pepper me up. That was all motivation to get better.

The student not only has to have clarity about the question, but attunement to the energy to know when is the right time to ask it.

You must know what it is you want; you must have clarity. You must know the general direction, but you can't have expectations about how it will look. You must know what you want but you can't focus too directly on it, or it pushes it away. You only get it by not directly fixating on it. There's a balance between knowing where you want to go and not being fixated on it. The more you are fixed and inflexible, the more you push it away. You can't tackle God and rip something out of God's hands. You must be like a cat. You want something but you don't seem particularly interested in it. You act a little wishy-washy about it even if you really want it. In your heart, you know that you want it. If you are inflexible, if God wants to give you more, or something different that is more appropriate, God can't do that.

Maintaining Inner Neutrality

If anything was bothering me when I went on duty, Swami would feel it, then it would bother him. So, when I was around him, I had to be very careful of my interactions with people and other students so I didn't get upset.

Another angle for me to be aware of was how my attitude toward someone could influence his opinion, especially early on. If I had a negative feeling towards someone, sometimes he would ask me about it or just act on it. I did not want him to have to process my reactions, and I did not feel it was fair for me to influence him. No matter what my opinion of someone or a situation, I knew I didn't have the whole picture. The other part was, I had no idea about what Swami was doing with any individual or situation. I felt I only had a small window into things, I didn't want to influence him because I knew that I didn't really know. So, I tried hard not to say things in any direction other than what I knew to be true, literally to just present the facts. For me, it was extremely important to be totally neutral to not disturb or try to influence him with my personal opinions. Even my interactions with other students had to be neutral. If someone said something rude to me and it was bothering me, he could feel that. I couldn't let my personal feelings for someone color his opinion.

If Swami asked me something about someone, I always told him the truth. Of course, he got as much of a reflection about where I was at as about that person. He could be confirming something that he already knew. Swami didn't waste his energy, if he asked, he had a reason. I preferred to say good things about people, but I always tried to be honest.

Sometimes if someone sent a letter to Swami, he would have me read and pick out the most important parts. The way I would interpret or present it would influence the response he would give. I would recognize and try to monitor my inner reactions. You could never change Swami's mind, but you could flavor things. I had many interactions with Swami where I didn't think some things were important to him that were. So, I tried to be neutral in how I presented things.

Previous attendants had pushed their opinions on him, and it had been hard for him. They tended to present things to him along with their opinions of people. To some degree, it would color his reactions. At first, Swami didn't have a good understanding of Western psychology, so it was possible to influence him. He had to learn how Westerners thought. Later, he was much more in tune with Westerners and could read between the lines. In the beginning, it was a little harder for him.

Swami complained about two female attendants who tried to influence him with their opinions and judgments about people, and the way things should be handled in the ashram. In truth, they felt they knew better than he did; they had their own agenda about how things should be handled in the ashram. They felt Swami didn't know about real-world things, but they did. He would complain that they were wasting 50% of his time and wanted to run the ashram. He asked for help from a group of close students because it had wasted so much of his time and energy. They were injecting negativity about others to try to raise themselves up in his eyes and solidify their position. If things didn't go their way, it took a lot of time and energy to try to set them right and handle their emotions and upsets. Because of Swami's love, it was difficult for him to remove them from his service, so he asked a group of students close to him for their help because it was disturbing his mission and time was running short.

It was essential for Swami to have time to relax, have quiet time and de-charging time, and they were sucking his energy and diverting his attention. That is where my desire to not pull on his energy with my own stuff came from. I saw how disturbing this was for him, and I knew it was not serving him. It was important to just give him the facts about what I knew and not color it with my opinion. If he asked for my opinion I would share it, but mostly he did not. I made a conscious choice to not use my closeness with him to try to command on his time or to push my personal agenda with him.

Lunch on Mandir steps

Care and Feeding of an Avadhut

Feeding

If you didn't remind Swami to eat, often he wouldn't eat. Early on, he was better about eating. That was one of the things I had to pay attention to. When his food came, I had to tell him his food was there. Often, he didn't eat for some time, so I would remind him. Sometimes he would get irritated but would eat. You never knew. It was part of my job, so I had to take the chance. I would say, "Swami, it's been eight hours and you haven't eaten. Would you like to eat?" You had to approach him delicately and respectfully and take the risk of annoying him.

In the Indian tradition, you don't eat before the guru. If you are serving him, your being hungry reminds you that the guru is hungry. Near the end of his life, Swami would tell me to take some of his food. But if he hadn't eaten any, I wouldn't take any. By that point, I could go for a long time without eating. He had already eliminated my need to eat regular meals, so it wasn't a big deal. It was just one of those things that was ingrained in me, to think of him first.

When the energy went high, Swami wouldn't eat. In the early days, on the Full and New Moons when thousands of Indians would come for his darshan and blessings, he just didn't eat. He said he could live on coconut water; that was the minimum to keep him going. He would go until he finished all the interviews. He could be up all night.

In the ashram, he would almost always eat whatever was offered. He always ate curd rice, which he really liked. If he ate nothing else, he would eat curd rice. You had to put salt on the plate next to the curd as well as lemon or mango pickle. The curd was freshly made from buffalo milk, which is thicker and creamier than curd made from cow's milk.

Swami had multiple Indian women cooking for him. If three women sent containers with food and he just ate food from one, that would get back to the other two women and he would feel bad. That's when he said it was our job to eat his food! Especially, if Swami's mother or wife cooked for him, we would be sure to eat it to protect him. If all the food disappeared, the women would see their food was gone, they were happy and couldn't tell if Swami had eaten it or not!

One essential thing about taking care of him was to keep things familiar and comfortable. He liked consistency. If he wanted to change things, he would just come in and say he wanted it a different way. You had to do it the way he wanted. Then the next day, he could come in and change it again. Again, we would do it the way he wanted. He was working with people's egos. My job supporting him was just to do what he wanted, not what I thought was best. The point was to make it easy for him.

I would line up some snacks on his desk in a particular order, the same way every day. I got bored, so I thought he might be bored. So, I tried putting everything in a different order. Moments later, I walked back into his office and saw he moved everything back where I usually put them! That's how he wanted it. I couldn't be egotistical about it; it wasn't about me. It was for him. I never tried to move them again!

One of the other attendants was kind of hyper about serving Swami, jumping every time he said something. There was quite a contrast between the two of us. My experience was that you needed to be calm, you couldn't be wound up with nervous energy when you were around him. If Swami gestured that he wanted more food, the attendant jumped up out of his skin. If I served Swami, I brought the serving bowl over and gently put it on Swami's plate. Swami didn't like the smell of the food, so you had to stay a little away.

One day, when Swami asked for more, the attendant walked over and grabbed the plate out of Swami's hand! He had been on duty for a while but didn't know some basic things. It was funny to me, he felt that anytime Swami asked for anything you had to run. Not everything was an emergency. For whatever reason, Swami was comfortable with this person. I tried to help him, but I wasn't going to lecture him about everything. Swami was comfortable with him. If I had grabbed the plate like that, Swami would have hit me with it!

When we traveled abroad, he would carry jars of his mother's homemade Indian pickles and powders everywhere we went. He wouldn't travel without them. It was a serious thing if they were forgotten! They were precious cargo in his carry-on bag. But there was a price to pay, and Swami was willing to pay it. The pungent jars of condiments caused him to be pulled over by security every time he entered the US. The pungent smell of spices was everywhere. Explaining it was always interesting.

He could live on just Indian pickles, powders, and cooked rice. He especially liked groundnut peanut powder. Generally, he didn't eat anything but Indian food when he traveled abroad. He wanted vibrations of the food to be like what he was used to. If you gave him Western food, he would just stir it up and not eat. I never saw him eat Western food.

We got better at getting him food when he traveled. The people traveling with him would arrange Indian food privately cooked, but this didn't always work out. Just having Indian food wasn't enough; it also depended on who cooked it. He was extremely sensitive to the vibrations of the person who cooked his food. Even if he was really hungry, he wouldn't touch the food if he didn't like the vibrations. He could tell without tasting it. The thing was, he was eating the karmas of the cook who prepared it!

He always wanted fresh coconut water available, no matter where he was. If he didn't eat, he would just drink that. It was harder to get abroad. The first time I was with him in America, I had to get coconuts, hold them between my feet, and hammer the nail to get the water. He would drink that. He could live on that for a few days.

I learned to serve Swami from Chitty, who had done it for a long time. How it should be done was instilled in me. One thing, serving him food you had to put it on the plate in the right order, and it had to have the right aesthetic. Nothing could touch each other, anything with liquid had to be near the bottom so it did not mix with other things. I watched Chitty serve Swami for months before I served him. Even later, if Swami had multiple guests in the office, Chitty and the Indian staff would be outside. They would serve the food, put it on the plate, and I had to take it in and hand it to the people. I would go back inside and hang around while they were eating and would offer them more. If they ate everything, it was an indication they wanted more. If you offered it and they said no, but they didn't put their hand over their plate or physically move their plate away from you, you served them more. If they just said no, they were being polite, and you didn't listen to it.

Turns out that learning how to serve was a big deal. Chitty could handle up to four people easily. I appreciated the staff since they always knew what to put on the plate first, and what was the second course. Mostly, I knew that the curd

155

rice was last. Some of the other things I wasn't a hundred percent sure of. By the end, I knew Swami's food, but when it came to serving guests, that was more complicated.

There are tons of rules in Indian society about how you should behave around a guru. Swami didn't enforce a lot privately, but in public, he was stricter. It was a strong cultural thing in Indian society. Swami was very tolerant. He knew most of his students didn't know these things, nor did he really want a lot of them.

But I felt I should be aware of society's expectations when in public. If the Indian staff was around, they noticed. I watched the Indians interact with him and followed their example: how they served his food, how they approached him, how physically close they came. Learning by watching comes naturally to me.

If you were with him in private, it was different. If you were in the office with Swami, you had to sit properly. That meant feet on the ground. He was a stickler; he didn't let people cross their legs. If women were wearing *punjabis*, he was particular about how they sat in the temple. If I knew he was coming, I always put my feet flat on the floor. 'Perk up, no lounging, be awake, sit properly, and pay attention when he walks through.' No matter what I was doing, there was a part of me that was listening to what he was doing, feeling his energy. I was always aware, even if I wasn't focused on it.

All throughout my serving Swami he was breaking my attachments, including food. At one point, my friend, Shakti,[27] began cooking for me. Generally, around 11 am or so, I would go on duty. I would receive a call from the Indian staff when Swami was up. At noon, Shakti's daughter, Isa, would deliver her freshly cooked lunch in stainless steel *tiffins*. She would leave the food for me under the staircase leading up to the Jesus Temple.

When it was time to eat, I would sit behind the railing in the waiting room out of sight. If someone went up the stairs, I could be eating without being seen. Also, from there, I could hear if Swami called me. It was an excellent place to eat my meal but if Swami called, I would put it down and run to him. Not surprisingly, there were times when my food container arrived and suddenly Swami would have tons of busy work for me! He would give me all these things

---

[27] Kirsten Thompson.

to do. I could smell the food but never had time to eat it. That was the beginning of him breaking my attachment to food. It seemed obvious that he was doing it. It was consistent. I would walk by and could smell it but couldn't eat it, and I was hungry.

One day, Swami was sitting in his chair in the Jesus Temple with a small group. Swami saw Isa, Shakti's daughter, come up the stairs with a food container and asked why she was there. I told him that her mother had cooked me food and she was bringing it to me. He started to get upset, "They are spoiling you!" I said, "Yes, Swami, they are spoiling me so I can spoil you. They are bringing me food so I don't have to leave and can stay and take care of you." Then he got a huge smile on his face.

Bathing

Swami had a five-gallon bucket in his bathroom with a dipper. This is for an Indian bucket bath. He expected the water filled and at the proper temperature for a shower. You had to keep the water ready for him at any time. Once early on, Swami wasn't there, so I made the water a little bit warmer. He showed up and complained that it was too hot! I thought he would touch the water before he poured it and run a little cold water to get it right. But he didn't do that, he just scooped it up and poured it directly on. Whatever temperature the attendant made was the temperature he would use. He was really depending on me to get it right. Whatever the reason was he did that, it was kind of a shock to see that he was dependent on me for that.

Sometimes it felt like he was doing some of these things just as an exercise to develop my attention. It definitely did that. When I trained the new attendants, I taught them to check the bathwater every half hour whether he was there or not, to keep it at the right temperature. It was hard for people to understand why he couldn't just do it on his own.

Swami was also very particular about the toiletries in his bathroom. Everything had to be in exactly the right place, fresh and full. If the shampoo went down a quarter bottle, it had to be replaced. He only liked Indian brands; he did not like Western products. All the toiletries had to be in the same place every time. Immediately after he left the bathroom, it was cleaned, and the toiletries rearranged exactly like it was.

If Swami's shampoo bottle was empty, he would just quit shampooing his hair and wouldn't tell you he needed a new bottle! It was a weird thing; he just wouldn't say anything. So, you had to check all the containers. He was also particular about the expiration date. He wanted his toothbrushes changed often. Mostly he would throw them out the window. Then I would see there weren't any toothbrushes because he had thrown them out the window! Swami was funny that way. If he picked a pen and it didn't write immediately, he would just throw it in the trash. If he was on his northeast bed, he would throw it off the balcony!

Clothing

Swami would go through a lot of clothes. We were constantly scrambling to have enough clothes for him. Swami could take many showers a day, changing into fresh clothes each time. During big festivals, like Guru Purnima, he could easily take twelve showers and change his clothes each time! The Indians would also steal Swami's clothes from the clothesline! It's a big blessing to have clothes from a saint. There wasn't much we could do about that. Swami would also give his clothes away. When he visited Laytonville,[28] he would leave a huge suitcase full of clothes. He would leave with a dozen set of clothes and come back with three! He would come back with just his carry-on. He did that on purpose. It's a huge boon to make them available for students to meditate with.

Swami was very thin at first, then gradually got a lot heavier, then at the end of his life, lost weight. He got frustrated when his clothes didn't fit him. His pants snapped because they didn't have elastic, and had to be let out and taken in. I told him to just put on his fat pants! Then his pants were too big, and I had to punch more holes in his belt. He had a huge long belt, but since it was under his kurta, he didn't care. I kept punching holes as he got smaller. Part of the problem was that Swami liked his pants below his heels because he wanted his

---

[28] Now the Divine Mother Center.

feet covered. If he did that and was wearing pants that were too big, they would fall down! He didn't want to deal with that. So, we were constantly running out of clothes and constantly making more.

Swami's clothes were simple but immaculate. He wore white cotton pants with either a knee-length kurta, with or without a scarf, or with a short-sleeve button-down shirt. His clothes were crisp white, perfectly ironed, hung on hangers, and hand delivered by the ashram *dhobi*. Swami wanted clothes that were not stained, marked, or burned. He cared about how he looked and the way he dressed. We had to make sure the clothes on his rack were not stained or burnt. If you put it back on the rack without checking, you would hear about it.

We had racks of clothes and were constantly putting out new selections of clothes. We had a big rack of shelves with colorful scarves to choose from. I always felt a little weird about choosing for him. He had favorite colors and tended to wear the most bright yellow and orange, sometimes he liked the ones with metallic inlay. It varied. Often, I would stand at the top of the stairs in the Jesus Temple and look at him before he would go out. If he had loose threads on his scarf, or loose threads on his clothes, I would say something. He appreciated that. He cared about looking nice.

Life Around Swami

A quirk of Swami's personality was it always seemed there was a part of him that wanted some interaction. If he threw something towards you, he didn't expect you to just dodge it and drop it, he expected you to hit it back to him. Westerners weren't used to that. In certain circumstances, he would appreciate it if you hit the ball back to him, but only in the right circumstance. If he was upset and you caused it, it only made it worse. If he was in a jovial mood, he would appreciate it. You had to feel when it was appropriate.

Like the time Swami complained about his glass not being full. So, the next time I poured it to the very brim, then I walked in and set it down without spilling it on his desk. This is an example. He threw the ball to me, then I threw it back. It was an energetic tossing it back at him. He didn't say anything, he just looked at it then just looked at me. Not a peep, not a word, he just bent over to sip it since he couldn't pick it up. He didn't say anything! If you did it in the right way, he seemed to appreciate it.

Certain things, without any bad intention, I would throw back at him. It was a little game that could run, but you didn't want to get too caught up or attached to it. It could turn quickly. For me, there was always respect for Swami. I never wanted to do anything that irked him.

The longer I was on duty, the more I surprised Swami. He was amused by it. Usually, he was the one surprising everybody.

There were a few times I opened the living room door, and he was right there, just as he was reaching for it. You could see he was surprised! As I was up there longer, I could do that more, surprise him, or walk up and he didn't sense I was there.

He never wanted me visible to the students below. I was supposed to stay away from the edge of the Jesus Temple. I would go over to a part of the wall that was taller and look down, so people couldn't see me, but I could look for Swami. One day it sounded like he was coming but then didn't. I went to look over the side to see where he was, and he was right behind me! He said, "I am right here." He knew exactly what I was doing. I didn't even hear him; he was just there! He got a big kick out of that.

He was talking to our group before Mother Divine darshan and said we are going before God; you will have a direct experience of God. He told us we had to ask the Mother for something. The funny thing is, God knows us better than we know ourselves. We are asking something that God already knows we're going to ask. It's a kind of funny game.

As I was there more, I saw how busy he was, and how much he thought about his students. Before a program, the office would prepare books with information and photographs of the students coming in advance of the program starting. He would go through those. He looked at each student's picture and read their information. He asked for their birthday, parents' names, where they were born, what processes they had done.

Swami would make things seem like they just happened on the spur of the moment. But he did not operate that way. In reality, he planned things. He wouldn't talk about it so Maya couldn't stop it. Even when he was doing it, he wouldn't make a big deal of it. But usually, you could tell by his energy, which

160

would be super high, and sometimes he would get kind of edgy. I didn't know why but I could feel it, something was going on.

When he would appear in public, things that seemed so casual or offhand were prepared well in advance. Maya could come if he revealed what he was going to do, so he never talked about it. He just did his homework. He researched. He had an idea, then would make it seem completely spontaneous.

Swami was very disciplined and organized. He was on top of all things in the ashram. He ran a tight ship. Swami knew the value of money. Money didn't disappear, and he didn't throw it away. If he gave you money, he expected an accounting of all of it. He was tight that way. There weren't many people he would let handle money. Especially in the early days, he was strict about it. Later, he was a little more relaxed, but was always pointed.

Swami trusted me with money. He saw I was frugal; I didn't spend money freely. He never said anything, but I felt he appreciated that I wasn't free with his money.

People would bring him gifts, but he wasn't that interested. He would look at the things, and sometimes ask who gave it and I would tell him. Mostly he wouldn't even touch the stuff, he would just glance at it and wouldn't really care. Occasionally, there was something he was attracted to which he wanted around. You never knew what he was going to do.

Men's group to Shirdi, 2003

Men's group to Shirdi, 2003

Tirupati, 2003

Men's group, Sri Sailam, 2003

Men's group, Sri Sailam, 2003

Men's group, Hyderabad, 2003

Men's group, Hyderabad, 2003

On the road to Shirdi, 2005

Waiting for Swami, Tirupati, 2011

Travelling

Travelling with Swami was something. He took us to the most amazing places, and we got to spend time with him in power spots, airports, limousines over the Alps, crammed into his Mercedes. It was always an adventure.

Swami had wanted to go to Shirdi for many years, but Baba wouldn't give him permission to come. Finally, Swami got permission! Even Swami was tested by his master, Baba.

We flew to Poona to drive to Shirdi but there were no good rental cars available. Swami didn't want to wait for a better car, so we went with what they had... *really* slow cars. Painfully slow. They could only go about 45 mph! Swami was so antsy he asked the driver if he could drive. The driver said no. It seemed that Baba was testing his patience a lot before allowing him in Shirdi.

One thing Swami hated was to waste time, so he spent the entire five-hour drive on the phone talking to people.

One time they were doing a big clean-up of the ashram, and Swami made a list of all the things that needed to be disposed of. At the end of the day, he asked me for one of the items on the list. I told him, "No, you told me to get rid of it, so I got rid of it!"

He said, "You have to think for yourself, even if I tell you something you have to do what's right. You knew I was going to need it." I realized early that even if he said something, he was expecting me to think, not to just blindly do things. I had to apply this in other places, like when Swami was saying something about someone. I had to be able to think for myself, he is expecting more of me. Perhaps he is saying something in the moment and is distracted, whatever, I have to think ahead.

You have to be prepared, but unexpected things are still going to happen. Swami would ask for something I didn't know or want me to do something I had never done before. He did that almost every day. I had to figure it out.

What do I do when he asks me to do something I don't know how to do? Do I say anything? Swami wouldn't have any tolerance for that. He wanted you to figure things out and be resilient. Just do your best, don't make it a big deal. Don't put a huge amount of frivolous spinning energy around it. Just do your best to take care of it. Sometimes I would make a mistake and would have to go back and tell him, "I tried but it didn't work." Then he would grimace, and I would feel bad but still, I tried. "What do you want to do now?"

We have a brain; we have to use it. Swami expected that. He was not one to tell you every step of how to do everything. Try, figure it out. You have to at least try.

The thing with Swami was you always had to be ready for anything. One day, he told me we were going somewhere; I should go back to my room and pack my bag. He was in the Jesus Temple getting ready. I had to take care of a lot of things before I could even start to pack. I was getting things prepared when he came and said, "Ok, let's go!"

"Swami, I haven't packed yet! I didn't even make it back to my room!"

"Do you have your computer?"

"Yes."

"Okay, get in the car. We'll buy whatever you need." That was it. I left with nothing but what I had on me. Fortunately, I always carried a toothbrush in my bag. I got in and off we went! When we got where we were going and needed clothes, he sent the Indian staff out to buy some.

When Swami said, "Let's go," you better be ready!

Swami had a Mercedes SUV. Mostly we would travel at night. We used to put the back seat down and lay blankets and pillows so Swami would have a nice place to sleep for a long drive. It was very nice. The rest of us piled in next to him. You shouldn't touch him, but often three people could be lying down next to him. If someone wanted to roll over, all three of us would have to roll over. Then someone else would roll over; then we would all roll over again. This went on over and over for the five-hour ride.

You really had to have no expectations when travelling with Swami, about anything! Taylor[29] and I travelled with Swami to his apartment in *Tirupati*. Two longtime Indian devotees, Suri and Vani, had a place up above and Swami's apartment was downstairs. Swami stayed with them, so he sent us down to stay in his apartment. I was excited to have some time to rest in a comfortable place. It's a big deal travelling in India.

When we arrived, there was not a single thing in the entire apartment! No furniture, no chairs, no towels, not a bar of soap. We were sleeping on the stone

---

[29] Gary Taylor.

floor with nothing. We spent a couple of nights like that, then Suri finally brought some mattresses down.

One night, Suri came down and told us Swami said we were leaving. We should get ready right away and wait in the car. It was about midnight. We rushed and gathered our things, got the driver, and went down to the parking garage. The apartment building was built on stilts, so the garage was on the ground floor. We were ready to go. We waited. And waited some more. Every time the elevator dinged, we perked up, but it was not Swami. It was cold sitting. The driver just went to sleep in the back seat. Taylor and I just sat in chairs and waited. Finally, as the sun was coming up and it was starting to get warm, Swami came. We had waited until morning.

After we left Tirupati, I thought we were going back to his house in Kadapa. We went another direction to a big temple complex. I had no idea where we were. When Swami is in a temple complex, he moves quite fast, you have to zip along and push through people to keep up with him. Inside the complex, holy water came out of the rocks, filling the water tanks and pools with water. Swami went in the water. I had never been anywhere with him where he went in the water. He took his shirt off and went into one of the tanks. I was there holding his clothes.

It was cold, but he went into the water. After he came out, he got painted with the *Vishnu sign*. He let the priest draw the 'V' on his forehead, which was something I had never seen. He never let anyone touch him.

Another thing travelling with Swami, you had to be quick on your feet. For Swami's birthday, a group of us traveled to Tirupati with him. It was super crowded. Swami gave instructions of what to do, then went to the next place. Whoever heard the instructions would follow him. If you didn't keep up, you missed his instructions! I quickly learned that in a temple you have to keep up with him. If you didn't keep up, he would not wait. That is another thing with the energy, when the energy goes high, Swami got short, it was up to us to keep up. Swami gave the example of a baby monkey hanging onto the mother no matter what. With Swami it was the same way; you had to keep up.

You're going to the temple for energy reasons, not tourist reasons. There are things you need to do to receive the energy and blessing from the deities and power objects in the temple. You need to stay focused and have clarity, as there are so many things to distract you. The crowds, the noise, moving from one place to the next, can distract you from the real reason you are there.

As a rule, Westerners didn't understand that you only had to see or touch the murthi for seconds. Indians don't hang on for ten minutes, they receive the energy, say their prayer, and go. Connect, say your sankalpam and personal mantra, receive the energy, then go. I was kind of shocked at first when I saw how Swami did that. How quickly he would do everything in the temples and be zooming through. You had to keep up, or he left you in the dust!

When I finally got up to see *Balaji*, it was a big experience. The energy coming off Balaji was palpable. There were waves of energy radiating from him. At that time, you had to go through seven doors to get near him. At each doorway, the wave got more intense.

Another thing with Swami, you never knew what kind of situation you would wind up in. Mostly Swami wouldn't ask my opinion, but occasionally he would. One time we were in Kadapa, and he wanted to go to a wedding. It was going to be a huge wedding. He was worried about security, so he asked me about it, which was unusual. He asked me what I thought about him going without any security. I told him I wouldn't recommend it. So, we went anyway.

It was super crowded, super noisy, and there were thousands of people. Swami walked in by himself, and I was supposed to pretend I didn't know who he was. So, I was standing in the back, the only white person in the whole room! Everyone was looking at me and I didn't have anyone to talk to, I didn't know a single person. I stuck out like a sore thumb. Thank God no one asked me if I was friends of the bride and groom!

Sometimes Swami would send me off without him to do sadhana. A few times he sent me to Hampi with another student. He and I shared a hotel room. When the energy would get high, he would fidget and couldn't sit still. He would take his luggage apart and repack it; he had to do something. He would look at me, 'How can you just sit there?' I would look at him and think, 'How come you have to keep moving around?' It was irritating and jarring to me that he was constantly fidgeting and doodling. The higher the energy, the quieter and more inward I go. He was the opposite, the higher the energy, the more external he became. He had a hard time containing the energy. We finally decided we had to get separate rooms. We couldn't be in the same room; it was torture for both of us!

That's how we solved it; we would always stay in different rooms. I really liked him, but when the energy was high, we were each other's worst enemies. We were opposites in how we handled the energy. In the end, we respected each other's ways of being, didn't try to make each other different, and stayed in separate rooms.

When we traveled inside India, I didn't have a support staff to help. At the ashram there were people around, so I would get more breaks. When we traveled, it was mostly me and his drivers. I could send the drivers to get things, but they couldn't serve Swami. So, I was with him 24-hours, which made it difficult.

He didn't expect me to work more than he did, but he did expect me to work as much. He could go on two or three hours sleep a night, which meant I had to be able to do that too. He could go three days in a row without sleeping, without even lying down. All I could do was just keep going. I was pushed to exhaustion and beyond. I would ask myself, 'Can I physically withstand this? Can I actually do it?' My approach was that I just needed to make it through the next five minutes, the next hour, this day.

It's a different perspective when you start every day having no idea how long you will be working. When I went on duty, I never knew if it would be for hours or days. It was a surrender. I remember at the end of Swami's life, I looked at the clock and wasn't able to tell the hour hand from the minute hand. I thought, 'I've been here for days. It could be 10:00 at night or 10:00 in the morning!' I couldn't tell because my body was so tired. I even fell asleep standing up. I always caught myself within a couple of inches.

Supernatural Master

Experience of Shirdi Sai Baba

Swami gave us so many wonderful processes over the years. We had lots of experiences during those processes, to receive the energy and open a channel.

One night after Aarthi, Swami had me go to the Baba Mandir and meditate in front of Baba with his *padukas* on my head. I had to meditate for an hour with Baba's silver padukas on my head. I did this every day for many days; I don't remember how many. I really felt Baba's presence and had some wild visions!

One time Swami called a bunch of people to the Jesus Temple, then went around and gave shaktipat. When he gave me shaktipat, I noticed that his thumb was big and very coarse. Afterward, Swami asked if anyone had looked. No one had because he had said to keep our eyes closed. He said it was Baba who had given shaktipat! If we would have opened your eyes, we would have seen Baba! I had noticed that his thumb was huge and coarse but didn't open my eyes.

One evening, in the beginning days of the ashram, Swami called three of us to his living room. He was sitting in his rocking chair and started talking with odd mannerisms. He was different. He started telling us things about our souls. Mostly what I heard was this was my last life. I was so excited I didn't hear much of the rest of what he said. Nityanandaji remembered that he told me I would be done with shakti processes, and I should just practice bhakti.

Only after we left, did we realize we weren't talking to him, it was Baba. That is why he seemed different! He was channeling Baba, which means that Baba was in him.

Nityanandaji said, "Baba said some beautiful and amazing things to us. He spoke to each of us with a message. We were there as a witness for the other. I've known you since before meeting Swami, I already loved you, and knew you would be a part of my life forever. 'You are a gem.' Those were Baba's words."

Managing in the Miracle Energy

A lot of mistakes would happen in the high process energy because some people got spaced out and lost their ability to think clearly. Mostly I seemed to be able to operate well in the energy and think clearly. If I did make a mistake, I didn't make a huge deal about it.

Swami would give a simple process to students, then they would make a mistake and go back to him and ask him to fix it. As a student, you have to win the guru's confidence. If you can't follow simple instructions, it kills their inspiration for helping you more. You had to be confident and competent in the high energy to do it.

I was kind of slow with learning mantras, and not the best at memorizing them. If we were doing a process and Swami would say to do a particular mantra, I could count on my brain not working. I would depend on someone else starting them, then I could jump in. In certain ways, my brain would go offline in high energy, but I could stay present and pay attention when the miracle energy was present.

My whole approach to being around Swami was to manage my own energy so it didn't disturb him. Naturally, I had ups and downs, but I knew what to do to stabilize myself, especially in the high energy. I would decharge, or be quiet, which is my natural inclination anyway. When the energy was high, I cultivated more silence. It really helps me to manage high energy. I got a lot of practice, not just when Swami was doing miracles.

Being around Swami meant living in a kind of a paradox. He was constantly feeding you high shakti, whether he meant to or not, just by his presence. And that constantly pushed you toward an imbalanced state. It was my motivation to take care of him that helped me digest the energy in a balanced way, otherwise I wouldn't have been able to. I would have gone into a negative place. I learned some lessons fast about what would happen if I didn't stay balanced.

It was harder when I was extremely fatigued. It was important to handle my inner world under any condition. It's not possible to feel secure and happy all the time. You have to integrate whatever state you're in. It's way easier if you're rested and fresh, if you're tired it's a whole other level. There were so many opportunities to practice maintaining my energy in a smooth way in the middle of a lot of things going on. That took years of practice; it didn't just happen.

It was amazing training to learn to maintain equilibrium in any circumstance.

When the energy went high during a miracle or any high-energy process, people would react differently. Some would go kind of brain-dead. They just stood around, they couldn't move, they couldn't think. They were out, nobody was home. As an attendant, I would have to watch for those people to help them keep up with their group. They would forget instructions. They would disappear and wander off. When a process was running you had to be careful about who was doing what.

One time Swami was in his office, it was a typical evening, there was a group in the temple meditating. It was a fairly big group; the group leader was German. My job as an attendant was to know who the group leader was.

He would call a group, the group would wait, then before he would talk to them, he would always ask, "Is everybody here?" One of the responsibilities of the group leader was to keep the group together and know if they were all there. The group leaders were generally more experienced students. If there was a process, I would give instructions from Swami to the group leader. It was up to the group leader to have the participants follow instructions.

One group was meditating in the Jesus Temple right outside the office. Swami was sitting in his office when somebody in the group coughed. I heard it, and Swami heard it. He told me, "Tell the group leader to take care of that."

The group leader reluctantly got up to talk to the person. I went back to the living room; I didn't say anything to Swami. He looked like he was meditating or concentrating. A few minutes later the coughing started again. This time Swami said, "Take care of that person or the whole group has to go, and the process is finished."

I walked back out and told the group leader to take care of it. She really didn't get why it was so important. She didn't understand that if Swami was disturbed the whole process was ruined. He was the process!

Once during a large program, there was a big group meditating in the garden. Swami was working with them. He told me to go out and get one of the group leaders. This was a common way that he worked during large programs. He would divide people up into smaller groups and work with them.

When I went out to the garden everyone was meditating, but I found the person and we went upstairs. Immediately, Swami told me to go back to get another group. I ran right back out and had to find the person. Once again, as soon as I got back, he immediately told me to go and get another group. I ran out again. Swami was going faster than I could get the groups up there. When I returned again, he told me, "Go get everybody. Hurry up!"

Once he opened a channel, he could only keep it open for so long, that was why he was in a hurry. People didn't understand that. They were irritated, thinking I was disturbing their meditation! People would tell me that I was ruining their meditation, or that my energy was erratic or disturbing. They didn't understand that Swami was waiting, and they had to hurry up! They didn't understand that when Swami was ready to go, you had to be ready or you were going to miss it.

I am sure that sometimes I was curt with people, but if people weren't responsive, Swami's frustration would escalate so I had to escalate to try to get them to listen. I knew this was their big chance to interact with him and do a process with him, I didn't want to do anything to disrupt that. But they didn't understand they had a window and they had to jump through that window, or they wouldn't make it. Often, I would have to be the one looking like the bad guy.

The idea is to be a clear neutral channel for what Swami was saying, to not spin it up or not downplay it. If Swami was getting irritated, I had to tell people to hurry up, Swami was waiting. For me, part of respecting Swami was respecting his time. We needed to follow Swami's timing since he was always following the energy.

Manifesting Gemstones

One night in the Jesus Temple, there was a small group of people who had not been to Penukonda before. The lights were turned down. When the miracle energy is present, it has a distinct quality. You can feel it if you have been around it. It's strong and can be kind of thick, dense energy. I could feel something going on with the group that Swami was working with. He asked me to get his bed. He would sleep on the marble floor in front of Jesus (statue) on just a towel or a thick fleece blanket.

I could feel the miracle energy. When the miracle energy is present, it took all his concentration. He had no tolerance for talking; he would be sharp with his instructions. He was quite sharp with me then, and I understood why; I could feel it. He had me hurry and get the blanket to make his bed in front of Jesus. I put it down the way he normally liked it when he slept there, but then he said, "No, not like that." I moved it another way, then he said, "No not like that." I could feel he was super irritated, but I didn't understand. I literally had no idea what he wanted.

He didn't want to sleep on it, he was manifesting something and wanted it to land on the blanket! He wanted the blanket folded in half, so it was a square, but I didn't know that. One of the people in the group understood what he wanted and ran up and folded the blanket into a square. Someone in the group told me later that he manifested the gemstones onto the blanket!

Supernatural Smoke

I was walking towards the Mandir, as a big program was about to start. I was late. Everyone was already seated in the Mandir. Swami was in his swing and saw me walking by. He called me over and told me to fill the *dhoop pot* and put it in the temple. The dhoop pot holds hot coals that you drop incense called *sambrani* in to purify a space with smoke.

It was a black clay dhoop pot. I had seen it done by the priests, but Swami had never asked me to do it. I went into the temple and got it on Baba's stage where it was sitting, then took it out to the dhuni and cleaned out the pot. There was a tool to get the coals out of the dhuni and put them in the dhoop pot. If you wanted it to go a long time, you had to fill it to the brim. I filled the pot with coals, shook it to get everything down, then put just a little bit of dhoop on top. If you put too much dhoop on, it overwhelms the coals and they don't smoke very much. I put a little bit on the coals then left and went back outside.

Before long, the whole Mandir was smoked up! It got thicker and thicker and thicker. It was supernatural, there was no way the amount of dhoop I put on there could make that much smoke. You could see the smoke pouring out of the doors and windows and lots of people were coughing! I thought, 'Holy cow, I didn't put that much on!' Swami just sat at the swing. I was super shocked, then I realized it wasn't me. There was no way I could have smoked up the Mandir like that.

Sambrani dhoop is used to clear negativity from the mind. Swami waited until the smoke started to dissipate which took 20 minutes. Then he went in and started the program.

A Group Manifests Atma Lingams

There was a group that Swami named the Yellow Scarf group. I think it started in Germany, but I am not sure. They started doing processes as a group. It was a big group, maybe 60 people, that came to the ashram a couple of times.

I was on duty in the Jesus Temple when Swami was preparing to do something. He didn't tell me what they were doing, which was generally the case. But this process was kind of Indian style, the practical details were not thought out. It was a good thing I was there to help him.

Swami had ice and wanted warm water. There was a lot of ice on the altar in front of Mary, a few big tubs of it, which was unusual to see in India. Then he wanted warm water. He had a five-gallon bucket in his bathroom, so I used that. I could feel something was going on because when his energy was high, he got curt and didn't want to talk. So, you had to be alert. The energy was really high, and people were responding to it, mostly they were a little out of it and confused.

After I got the water, Swami told me to go to the living room. When I first went on duty, anyone around saw what he was doing. As the years went by, he only wanted the people who were participating around unless he asked. It wasn't a problem for me. If he said don't come out, I wouldn't come out.

I had no idea what this group was doing. They were waiting downstairs. He had some of them come up to the temple to do their process. He did something, then needed more water. One bucket had cold water, the second, warm water. I had to carry two buckets for each person. I asked Swami if he wanted me to stay and help, he said no. But then after one or two people went, he called me back to help with bringing more water.

I had to go into his bathroom to fill the buckets, then carry them out to the temple; some water spilled on the polished marble and was super slippery. While carrying the buckets, I saw Swami put some ice in one bucket. Again, he told me to go away. So, I stayed in his bathroom since I figured I would need to refill more buckets.

I was in the bathroom and heard him giving instructions, then people moving about, so I went back out to get the buckets, carried them back, dumped them out, refilled them, put them in, and then back to the bathroom. What it evolved to was, I would hear him give instructions, hear the commotion, then he would yell, "Next!" and that was my cue to appear; I would go out there. Somebody else was feeding the people up to him. They were bringing people one at a time and each would come in and do their process. That went on for hours. I carried two buckets for each person; I think it was 60 buckets of water! Of course, in the end I had to clean the temple from all the water too!

I walked back and forth over 30 times without falling. The next day I was sore. Afterward I heard that each person had manifested an Atma lingam!

At the beginning of the process, Swami's energy was curt. He didn't want to speak, he didn't want to answer questions, he didn't want to give instructions. That is always a clue that the high-shakti miracle energy is running.

Some or most of the people who birthed the lingams had no idea what they were doing or the value of what they were doing. Swami gave so much to so many people that had no way of knowing the value of what they received. But he gave it, nevertheless. They had no idea what they were getting!

His Sankalpam

One time we had to do 41 days of fire pujas. Swami wanted us to focus on calling the feminine deities. The Brahmin priests also wanted to call the associated masculine deity. One of the male students in the group freaked out. He made a big show at the puja, berating the priests because they were calling the male consorts behind the female deities. What the priests said is you always call both, since they always come together; *Lakshmi* doesn't come without her consort! This student thought the priests were making a mistake. He was trying to tell the priests how to do their job, based on his misunderstanding. I asked Swami about it, and he said it doesn't matter what the priests do, it is the sankalpam behind it, and it is his sankalpam that is driving it. I asked if I should tell this other student to be quiet, and Swami wouldn't say anything either way. I did go back and tell the student to let the priests do their job.

Swami talked the hidden mechanism, if you want Shiva, call his consort but you don't necessarily call directly. Even beyond that, who the priests were calling was less important than Swami's sankalpam. Swami was clear about that; in some ways it didn't matter what the priests did because it was Swami behind it. He didn't even come to the pujas, he just put his energy behind it. Swami indicated that it didn't matter who did the puja; it mattered whose energy was behind it. He said, "I don't need to be at the fire the whole time. If I think about it, my energy can be there, I can send my energy to it."

Researching the Creation

Swami was a researcher on the creation. He didn't accept everything blindly without testing it himself. He said he never gave out practices unless he had experienced them himself first. Also, he didn't want us to follow spiritual beliefs blindly.

It was a *lunar eclipse*, all the murthis had to be covered as they do in all temples in India. In the ashram, people were told to stay in their rooms. I had to go on duty anyway. Swami was at the Dwarkamai. Another attendant and I were looking down from the Jesus Temple when he called us over. Swami was standing under the eave of the Dwarkamai roof, staying out of the lunar eclipse moonlight. He told me to get him an umbrella. "Nobody is supposed to go out," I said.

He replied, "It's ok for you."

We had to walk with him holding an umbrella over him so moonlight didn't hit him! It was an experiment. He was going out to see what it felt like, to understand why they cover all the murthis in the Indian tradition. An eclipse was supposed to have negative effects.

What he discovered was it was not negative energy. It's just a lot of energy. People may not be able to handle it, which is why they cover the statues. Then he had us walk in the moonlight. We were both laughing, 'How come it's ok for us if you can't go in it?' If something went wrong, I knew he could fix it. Maybe he was experimenting on us, too. It didn't really take two people to hold an umbrella. But our personalities were opposites, so he may have wanted to see how we each handled being under the eclipse energy.

Whatever he had learned in that experience he utilized that evening in a group process. He called everyone to come to the Mandir with all of their power objects. He had never done that before and never after this one time. We washed our power objects in an abhishek in front of Baba. As the objects of each person were being washed, waves of energy poured into the Mandir. The energy was unbelievably high.

No one except Swami had an idea how many power objects he had given people. It was really something to see. There must have been sixty people with their objects, and some came with lots!

Swami had hardly given me any. I had the same feeling as I always had; he gave me what I needed. Whatever I am going to do or however it works out, I don't need more. I could choose to be unhappy about it or I could choose to be happy about what I did get.

I spent lots of time around Swami, maybe more than anyone else. When Swami gave processes to everyone in the ashram, I never had to do them. I felt, 'You are around the biggest power object, you don't need to do anything.' I was around him, that was everything.

Thinking for Yourself

I spent time getting Swami's remotes all set up. Most of the time they worked, sometimes not. There was a help menu, but Swami didn't have the patience for it. When he wanted it to work, he wanted it to work right away. I told the attendants to look at the help menu and use it.

Generally, before Swami went into his office, I would turn the stereo on, make sure everything was working, and have music playing so he could change it if he wanted. If you were slow and he got in the office first and the remote didn't work, it was a big deal. Sometimes he would get in and would push the button and it wouldn't start. If I was off duty, the attendant on duty would call and say it wasn't working. I tried helping them over the phone, but generally they were too nervous and Swami was getting upset, so I would just walk over and fix it.

When I got there, Swami would be sitting at his desk and I would ask his permission to take his remote. Generally, I could fix it through the help menu. If I needed the remote, I asked his permission, although if he was upset, he would just hand it to me as I walked through the door, usually with a disgusted look on his face.

Then I would turn my back to look at the components. He was usually sitting behind me and saying all the wrong things to do! Then I would just tune him out; he was just background noise. I would just concentrate on getting it working and when it was working would just put the remote back on the desk. If I listened to him, he would have made it worse. That is what he did with the other attendants. They would get incredibly flustered when he told them what to do. Sometimes he was right, but often he was wrong. If I listened to him, it would take longer. I had to tune him out. It's a simple example, but it just shows that Swami expected me and needed me to think for myself, not just blindly do what he said.

Photo by Terry

On the Jesus Temple verandah

Jesus Temple, 2010

PART FOUR:
THE MASTER AS SCULPTOR

Swami with students

Why Avadhuts Behave as They Do

When the saints throw rocks and yell at you, they're not trying to hurt you. They know you're a purely innocent guy, that your soul is just a small candlelight, it's not enough dazzling light to remove the darkness of your mind. Through that screaming and yelling and throwing, it means they're putting your mind in control, to bring it back under your soul level. In their inner meaning, they're working on your soul, "Hey, wake up and get stronger." Even though you have to run away, later on, one day, you'll come fast back to his feet. That's for certain.

-Sri Kaleshwar

Swami explained the reason why avadhut saints behaved the way they did. Baba would get angry and scream at people, demand money. They behave like that for a reason. Swami would ask, "Is Baba just crazy, or is something else happening there?" He explained what souls like Shirdi Baba and Bhagawan Nityananda were really doing even though it looked terrible.

Same with Dattatreya, he's the purest being there is, but his behavior appeared to be terrible. A crippled man came to him for healing, and Datta just kicked him! But he was healed. Their actions are completely in their own realm. You can try to understand, but you have to be in their state of consciousness or just have faith in their Divinity. It's a real testing for people around these beings to see who really has that faith. Swami tested that, Baba did too.

People didn't think Swami could see through what they were doing. He found his own way to balance the karmas and give the right judgment for that person. Some people didn't ever seem to understand.

Swami acted this way with big donors who never came back. They expected certain treatment from him, instead, he treated them as students, but they couldn't see what he was doing. I learned it was best not to say anything when it happened to them. Even if I wanted to, I could not interfere or help them understand, there was backlash. It was their test and their process with Swami, I could not interfere, but I saw it happen over and over.

Swami worked intensively with a small group of people. He was very involved in every aspect of our lives. It was so intimate and personal the way that Swami worked with those close to him. He knew exactly what was inside each person, where the problem was, and knew how to get to it. He didn't work like that with very many people. You have to be very close to people to do that; you have to have that intimate relationship. With us, he was intense; he was chiseling us. It is hard to appreciate it when it is happening, the ego is always trying to protect itself. That was displayed in our resistance and reactivity. Now I can see and really appreciate the radical purification Swami did for us. It's not that there isn't fine-tuning, but now when working with people I see how much people need to purify. They don't know how much they need to purify. Now at the other end of the purification, I am so grateful. There is no way to get free of your ego without the master's help. These are all the things you hide from yourself, let alone having the person you care about most see them.

I saw how patient, compassionate, and committed Swami was in growing and training us. It took tremendous energy and time on his part. He pushed you, backed off, then waited for you to realize, then pushed you on that same thing to see if it was still there. He kept doing it until there were no more internal reactions. You were becoming a clean slate, free from conditioning. For me, it took years. He would push me, and I would have a huge reaction. A year later he would do it again, then wait for six months and do it again to see my reaction, to see if I was free. Then he would go onto the next one. It took so much love to do that with the people he loved. And at each one of those steps, you could blame or misinterpret his intentions; many people did.

Some people come to an ashram bringing their politics and having the same attitude with spirituality. They come with an attitude of 'you owe me'. Swami gave a lot of spiritual experiences to people; one could argue they weren't worthy of them. But that is what he was here to do, to give it out in the broadest way. In the past, you had to be qualified to receive what he gave. He pleaded with the *Divine Court* to allow it, as he told them the good people were getting destroyed by bad.

All these spiritual tools were given out, but most people were not eligible in the traditional sense. They were not purified, and that is why some funny stuff happened. Jealousy is a big problem in the spiritual world, especially in the world of power. *Adi Shankaracharya* was poisoned by someone who was jealous. They tried to kill Baba too, and look at Jesus. Swami had his own situation. The reality is the current world has a hard time not being jealous of such great people.

194

But we are on the brink of a new day. That is why Swami gave everything he could, even if we weren't fully eligible. The people who will use what he gave for good will outweigh the ones who are not eligible. He came into the middle of the darkest time and took on many terrible karmas of people. Like he said, he was a garbage man to take on these karmas. He really came to do a dirty job.

Swami didn't waste his time. He wouldn't have spent time with anyone if he didn't think they were worth it.

Chiseling the Ego

A rock can turn as a gem, no problem. I know how to make a sculpture on the rock, but it needs some hammering. After my hammering is perfectly done, then the world will start to throw flowers. First the rock has to receive the hammerings. If you get flowers on you, the chiseling is done.

-Sri Kaleshwar

We know the story about a sculptor who looks at a marble block and sees a beautiful statue inside the marble. We're like those blocks that are happy being a block. The master sees us and instead says we can become a beautiful statue. We say we want to be that beautiful statue. But to go from a block to a statue, those pieces must be chipped off. When the master starts chipping, we start complaining, 'Why are you hitting me?' If you really want to become what he sees you could be, you must give up those chipped pieces. Nobody wants to give them up. We are attached to those pieces; those pieces make us what we think we are. He is taking them because it is the only way you can reach your potential. We all fight the process to some degree. That is the nature of the ego, it attaches itself to what it identifies itself as.

But we really don't want to stay a block. Will blaming the person who is helping you the most make your process succeed? Okay, he just took a big sledgehammer and hit me as hard as he could, it hurt so bad. But look at what happened, my load was lightened. And why did he do that? What did he get out of it? It's hard work for him! You can complain about the blow, you can complain about the piece that was whacked out of you. He's doing you a favor.

You have to appreciate it; you have to see it for what it really is. You have to keep your heart open and keep your faith.

You want to be that beautiful statue, but will you stand for the work it takes to get there? When the hammer hits the block, when your world shatters, you pick up the pieces and go on. You are going to make it.

The thing you can't do is get upset with the master, it will only get worse. In every healing tradition, there are steps a student has to go through for personal healing and taking responsibility for their internal world. These are Human Potential Basics 101. Swami had much higher-level teachings to share. As he said, he came to teach Ph.D. information, not the ABC's. People that didn't know how to handle their own blocks generally did not do as well around him. I felt so grateful for the time I had in the Toltec tradition since I had done tons of personal cleaning of old beliefs.

Being exposed to my first guru at a young age started me on a path of self-discovery. I was asking the question, 'How does this world work, how does this reality work?' When I was studying with my guru, it was a bhakti path. I could meditate for hours but then be upset five minutes later. Bhakti seemed like a band aid, never really healing the infection. A good friend of mine got cancer, which forced me to look at things. I saw that I was going to keep repeating the same patterns until I learned the underlying cause and fixed it. Most people keep repeating the same mistakes. You get out of a bad relationship and change the superficial circumstances, but it doesn't change your experience since you pick the same type of person again and repeat the same patterns. My friend's dying was a wake-up call. He and I were very similar in a lot of mannerisms and in our lives. When he died, I realized it could happen to me, and I wasn't getting where I needed to go with my guru. I didn't know where that was, but I knew I wasn't getting there.

A lifetime of learning and seeking finally brought me to Swami. Why did I have those realizations that forced me to wake up? Was it soul capacity, or past life experiences? The truth is I don't know, but I was pushed outside of my comfort to continue the search. After David died, his wife gave me a lot of books on the emotional aspect of healing. If you feed yourself negative emotions, they can overwhelm your body. I have had that in my consciousness since then. Basically, it boils down to moving out of being a victim.

But when I went to Swami, it was a whole new level. I still got hooked by him and continued to have reactions that I needed to clean up and to let go of. But at least I had a framework to recognize what was happening, so I knew better than to blame him for my discomfort. Human beings are covered in emotional scars and wounds, which everyone thinks is normal, and often our friendships are based on who makes us feel good by not addressing our wounds. But your true friend is the one that points it out.

What Swami called 'blocks' are manifestations of the ego like anger, jealousy, pride, blame, selfishness, self-justification, unworthiness, insecurity, feelings of being left out, feeling you are right, impatience, hatred, greed. He had many methods of removing students' blocks.

A Skillful Master

Swami was a very skillful master. He was always working on his students and would work on as many people as he could at one time. He could hit so many targets with one arrow! I thought it was a channel he had. I never saw anyone do one thing and hit so many targets at a time. He didn't do it occasionally; he was consistent. He would be working in public not only with an individual, but would watch for other people's reactions to what he was doing. Who had compassion, or who was happy celebrating another's misfortune.

Another tactic was used for when someone wasn't strong enough to be worked on directly. If they couldn't handle Swami's energy being directed at them, he would give someone else a hard time about the same thing for the person who needed to hear it. He was pointing it out indirectly for them. Sometimes he would yell at me saying things that weren't true. When that happened, I knew it was for another person there but still always looked if there was something for me to see. We all have things that we hide from ourselves, he would give a big mirror to help you see them.

Mostly Swami would say things in an ambiguous way. If you had a block about what he was talking about, you could take it in a negative way. If you didn't have a block, you could take it in a positive way. Your reaction reflected where you were, not what he was saying. If he would say the sky is red, one person would throw their book down and yell that the sky was blue. The other person would say, yes, Swami, it's a beautiful red sky. He made a simple statement and your reaction to that statement reflected your internal world. He didn't have anything to do with it; you did it yourself. You had to see for yourself that your reaction was coming from you. Generally he wouldn't point that out, you had to figure that out for yourself. Most people didn't have any training in not being reactive, their reactions were obvious in their faces.

Sometimes I would see him say something controversial in a group and watch for reactions. He knew what he was saying was a hot button, and wasn't true, but he was fishing for reactions. It brought those internal reactions up. When a person reacts, there is some attachment to a belief, and when you're in a reaction you couldn't even hear what he was saying. And you weren't really reacting to what he was saying, you were reacting to the past, a trauma, or an attachment, an unexamined belief.

One time during a public talk, Swami singled me out. Afterward, a friend was commenting on how nice Swami had been. I insisted he was criticizing me. Luckily, I had recordings of that talk. When I listened to them, sure enough, she was right, that it was just in me, in my belief system, in my perspective. He wasn't criticizing me, but that had been my impression. Being able to hear the recording allowed me to hear that what he said was touching a damaged part of me that created a huge reaction. I realized that I hadn't even heard what he said, I was reacting to something inside me. I was able to see that. He had treated me with kid gloves, super delicately, super carefully, and still, I had a huge reaction. He wasn't creating that; it was all inside of me. He showed me it wasn't his criticism but my self-critical nature.

Sometimes people would push back on him. They could have an intense reaction and would try to push back. Usually, that wouldn't happen in public but in private. If you wouldn't look at yourself, you would project it onto him. It happens to healers all the time. When you help people, sometimes they blame you for what is going on with them. Swami was the biggest healer, so he received a lot of blame! He considered it a feather in his cap, that he was successful in his job if someone heaped blame on him.

Another method he used was to talk to someone about what they thought they were experts in. He would say something that was on the edge of their knowledge. They wouldn't believe it, but Swami would be right. But the other side was, he would know all these obscure things. I always thought he must have one of his angels telling him things! Whatever you thought you knew best, that is where he would challenge you. The stronger your reaction, the more it would encourage him. He wouldn't pick a neutral subject where you didn't have an opinion or a vested interest. He would deliberately pick a subject where you had a strong opinion.

The stronger your opinion, the more you would resist. The most important thing was not to resist. The more you fought back, the more he would push. He was constantly checking for our reactivity, our inability to have command of our internal world.

If he found one spot where he would get a rise, that was the spot he found all the different angles to get to. If you had any resistance, it only intensified.

Another method he used was to say unfavorable things about people in public. He watched your reaction. I would try not to react, especially in public. If he got a reaction from you, it just encouraged him to dig more. There was nothing you could do. Swami was always hitting multiple targets with one arrow. If he spoke badly about someone, he could see who was celebrating their disgrace. At times, I know he did this to protect me from a student's jealousy. It was his way of cutting their jealousy.

Swami had many ways of working with students, helping us recognize our blocks. He certainly wasn't doing it for his enjoyment. He did it to help us, to push us, to make us eligible to receive in the power channels. He was relentless. There are multiple layers of the blocks and making your way through isn't easy. If you didn't understand the basic mechanism, it was painful to be around him if you were stuck in a block. If you were open and willing to do the work, he would help move you through things fast, but you had to be honest with yourself and with him. Mostly, people tried to hide these things from him and from themselves.

I wouldn't have been able to succeed without the tools I brought with me. I saw people just hunker down more, rather than look at themselves. All that happens for that student is it gets harder. Ideally, he points it out, you work on that block, recognize it's in you, and move through with less and less internal reactions. Not because you are clinging or hiding it but because you no longer have a charge on it, then it is completely gone.

After one block was done, he would start on the next one, and occasionally, would come back and see if you had let go of it. If you had, it meant you were progressing and learning, you were becoming freer and happier. The truth is that all these internal impurities destroy our happiness and peace and as we heal them, we are happier and come closer to who we really are.

Swami pointed to things in me that needed to be healed. His job was to point them out. My job was to recognize them, and as I recognized whatever it was, it automatically had less hold of me. That is healing. Later, he didn't have much tolerance if you didn't take care of it. I had tools, and I had the awareness to look at those aspects in myself. It required continuous work. Some people could handle that kind of energy, and others couldn't. It was consistent, the ones who could or couldn't.

The stakes were high if Swami gave power to someone who was not purified, and they misused the energy. He was responsible for their karmas because he is the one who gave the knowledge. If he seemed hard on people at times, that was the reason. He had to be.

The Unfairness of the Avadhut Energy

I was away on a visa jump when Swami saw an Indian cardiologist who said his blood pressure was a little high. The doctor prescribed Nitroglycerin tablets. Years ago, I had worked with an older guy who took Nitro and described what it was like to me. By coincidence, I knew something about it. Nitro is a medication used to dilate blood vessels when having a heart attack. After you take it, you can get a screaming headache.

I didn't meet the cardiologist, but I noticed the new medication. I felt like it was the wrong medicine for Swami. I thought the doctor should be fired. He misdiagnosed Swami and should have never prescribed that medication. Swami took a tablet and got a raging headache. I told him this is what happens with this medication. I told him, but he didn't listen to me, since I was not a doctor. So, I had to call Constanza, his other Western doctor,[30] and tell her that an Indian cardiologist prescribed Nitro for him, and he had a bad reaction.

She was horrified and got really wound up. I told her she had to come talk to Swami since he wouldn't listen to me. She came and told him exactly what I

---

[30] Nityanandaji was his primary doctor.

had told him. She took the medicine away from him and said strongly that it was not the right medicine for him.

Swami was so happy with Constanza that he gave her an apartment! I had to laugh. This was later in his life. I had been taking care of him for years, and she swooped in and got a free apartment for something I had figured out! Swami was talking Constanza up to the other students, what a great job she was doing taking care of him. Of course, he never mentioned my part or said anything to me. By then, I wasn't surprised. With the avadhut if you are trying for praise or recognition, it's a recipe to crash, so I knew better.

The 'unfairness' of the avadhut energy is not an easy concept to understand or accept. He treated people differently based on an agenda they couldn't see. It is not visible; it is a soul-based criteria that only the master can see. As a student, if you just look externally, you will get upset. I could have so often had the thought, 'I have been here longer, I have been working super hard. Why is he putting his attention on them and not me? Why did they get that boon and not me?' Every person will have those kinds of feelings come up. They're natural. All of us have egos, all of us want recognition and acknowledgement. But will you see that in yourself? If you do, can you let go of it, and trust the master, trust that he knows what he is doing? Or hold onto that idea that it is not fair?

In the early days, Swami was learning about Westerners. He was researching. He would give something then watch what happened, watch how people reacted to see if their egos went up. He was testing, what are they going to do with this energy? How are they going to react? The master gives spiritual energy, shakti. If he gives it to people who abuse it, he has to pay the price. The way a lineage is created is one master teaching a student. The master tests the student for years before initiating them. What I saw was, people would come with their expectations and almost demanded things. That automatically disqualifies you.

You must be open-hearted and understand how the master gives. You have to know that the master is not going to give it to you on a silver platter. You have to do work to qualify for that. There are a lot of hidden elements that the master sees that we don't: your soul capacity, your dharma in the world, your previous lives, and how open your heart is.

Some people would get upset because they had been with Swami for years, but a new person came and Swami gave them a miracle experience. This seemed totally unfair. Maybe they have spent previous lifetimes preparing, maybe they have more in their soul bank account. It comes down to whether you trust the master to know who is qualified and who isn't.

There was an incident during a public program with hundreds of students attending from all over the world. Swami gave many miracle experiences in that program. During the Q & A of the last talk, a long-time student stood up and became aggressive with Swami in front of everyone. She said it was unfair that she and her husband had been there much longer and yet the newcomers got experiences of *aghora*. The woman was a teacher at his Soul University. As smart as she was intellectually, she was not spiritually aware. It is never advisable to be aggressive with the master. Swami just smiled and didn't say anything to her criticism.

What Swami gave and who he gave it to did not necessarily make sense. This could be extreme at times. Once he was doing a process giving people nine *strokes* with Mother Divine. Most of the people who got them were just casual visitors to the ashram, they weren't even students! They had no idea what they got or what to do with it. But they were given this extraordinary boon from Swami. We really don't see the full picture; he is seeing the karmas at the soul level.

We talked about the importance of taking responsibility for your mistakes. But the avadhut energy takes that one step farther – blaming you for mistakes you didn't make! Swami could take that a step farther by making that blame public. That is a great challenge to the ego! This would happen to me, getting blamed publicly for mistakes I hadn't made. I can say that often the responsible student was there and watched as I got blamed for something they did. They didn't fess up to their part. They were happy to let somebody else get blamed for their mistake. In one case, the person who had made the mistake was sitting right next to me! Not a peep out of him, not a word.

One energy mechanism running there was that I could take it. The person wasn't strong enough to receive the full energy Swami was throwing. I know he did this with some other students too, like Mataji and Nityanandaji. He was using them to work with other students. In public, he blamed them for things they didn't do. He would watch the reactions of the others around. Would they be happy? Would they speak up and admit their mistake? Would they be able to see the truth of what Swami was doing? Did they realize that Swami knew? Only a mature spiritual student could see what Swami was doing.

So, yes, the avadhut is not fair. It is not fair to our egos, belief systems or blocks. But it is completely fair in the realm of our soul development. The avadhut energy will seek for and push up your craziness to show you where it is. Of course, it is not pleasant, but you are not being picked on. The truth is, what you are carrying has to be purified to lift your soul. You can take it as criticism, harshness, or meanness. The master is there to crush your ego. The more you hold onto it, the harder it is. The master will intentionally create situations to push you and to see where you will crack. He will find the very thing that you have the strongest attachment and resistance to. If you were holding onto things, then it was painful. As Chogyam Trungpa said, "The master is there to insult you!"

He took away external reference points. He gave me no place to position myself, to see what was happening. Mostly he cut me off and isolated me (from other people) for that same reason. The other people couldn't see what was happening to me, and I couldn't see what was happening to myself. I would have been the first one to quit and go off by myself and have a happy life. He didn't give me that choice.

The Master's Leelas

I would usually put some music on in Swami's office when I was getting it set up for him to have people over. I would choose something quiet, just to have something playing when he came in. He could easily change it to something else if he wanted. He would usually never turn it off, he wanted music playing and wanted it ready. I had a good idea of the things he liked best and would choose. So, if he came in and chose certain songs, I knew it was for a reason, because he did not typically listen to those himself.

One technique he used to get a reaction in people was to play certain video songs when he had students relaxing with him in his office. One of his favorites for this purpose was *Loka Loka Loka*. It was racy by Indian standards. There was a scene of a woman dancing which he would play when certain people were around. He would put something on then look at me, like watch this! Generally, you could easily see who would react. He would often get a rise out of the women with that one. There was another of an Indian woman dancing in skin-tight shorts shimmying away. He knew he would get a reaction.

Of course, Swami would act completely innocent, saying we are having a party. For years, he teased Mataji with off-color statements to see what reactions he could get from her. One night, the siren in the movie sashayed about in a slinky red dress. As we were watching it, Swami told Mataji he was going to have a red dress made for her like the woman in the movie! Then he was going to put a picture of her on his website! She got it quickly. "Thanks, Swami. When can I go to the tailor in Bangalore?" Swami smiled.

People had a lot of ideas about how Swami should act. Watching racy Indian movie scenes was not on that list. When the people came in and a song like *Loka Loka Loka* was on, they had no way to know that was not what Swami normally listened to, that he had a special reason for having it on when they were there. But I knew.

Another way that Swami would work with people's blocks was by teasing and joking around. Swami loved to play; he would tease people to show affection. He would say something you didn't expect, and then he would watch your reaction to see where you were at. He could do it with one line! It made you feel close to him if he was playing with you or teasing you, if you weren't reactive. He would say, "I only tease people if I love them." But sometimes he would hit a nerve or it would be something you wanted to hide, but everything was fair game. Ego death is not an easy thing. It is a slow cutting, but he loved it. He really seemed to enjoy it. If you could get over yourself, you could enjoy it too.

Sometimes Swami would directly work on people's blocks by amplifying them. There was one student who was very fearful. Swami kept telling him that he was going to put him in the Dwarkamai with a rope of mice tied around his waist, then a cobra would be let loose! Every few months Swami would bring it up again. He was bringing up this guy's fear so he could face it and wash it out.

There were times that Swami would focus on someone, then look at me as if to say, 'Do you see what I am doing?' He never said anything, never explained. He wanted me to see and understand how he was working with people.

Sometimes he would tell the same story numerous times. If he didn't get a rise out of you, he would embellish it more each time. Supposedly one-time Mataji went home and turned his picture around because she was angry with him. Swami must have told that story fifty times, and each time he embellished it and got more and more elaborate. He said you only get angry with someone you love. He used the story to show the students that no matter how upset you get with the master, you can't escape that relationship.

Swami loved to make people get on the scale. He would have me step on the scale to wake it up. He would have everyone in the room get on the scale. They would say the number and Swami would say whether they had to lose or gain weight. Mostly for Western women, it was traumatic. But maybe for the men too. One time I got on and Swami told me that I had to lose weight. The next time, he told me I had to gain weight. Basically, I weighed the same both times! Either way, I thought, 'I eat once a day, I am running around like a chicken with its head cut off, my weight will be what it is.' One time he had the group in front of the Mandir on the slates and had everybody get on, then announced everyone's number!

With women, in terms of handling the energy, because of their Womb Chakra they can gain meditation power faster than men. But for women, it is more of a challenge to hold the energy. One way you can hold more energy is if you are heavier. He wanted women to be what we would consider heavier by American standards. He told several female students to gain weight. Some women tried but had a hard time gaining weight. Another student was overweight and terrified of the scale. She had been browbeaten about as a child and was insecure about it. A whole range of emotions got stirred up in everyone who was there. That was the point.

It was interesting to see the other side of that. There was a policeman who came to the ashram with his wife who was on the big side. Swami had them both get on the scale! His wife just hopped on with no anxiety at all. If she had been a Westerner, she would have had a different reaction. It was interesting to see that she had no concern about the number. Generally, Western women were afraid of the number on the scale, whether it was too much or too little. In the Indian culture, having a little more weight was not a big deal. They don't have a fixation with being thin like in the West. Telugu actresses at that time tended to be a little heavier. The movie ideal was more rounded. Swami was a proponent of that, he said many times he couldn't see how the West was fixated on stick women.

Satsang: Handling Your Blocks

Virtual Ashram, 2021

Shalini: You mentioned that Swami would sometimes say you were a failure. How did you handle that? When talking about blocks, you said, "If you're not willing to look at them yourself or take care of them, you could spend the rest of your life blaming people outside." How did you take care of them? Was this part of your daily review?

Terry: Sometimes what someone is saying and what you perceive is completely different. Often, you're just reacting from past traumatic events in your life. You're not reacting to what's happening; you're reacting to a past event. To clean it up you must go back to those traumatic events and review what happened, to let go of it, forgive yourself to live more in the moment and not always be reacting. That's quite a process. Swami said to do it every night before we went to bed. Some teachers call it recapitulation or witnessing. You go back through your day and review incidents to see if you could have changed something about what you experienced. Basically, that was it; every day before going to bed, review to see what you could have done better. I used this practice when things came up for me at the ashram. My prior Toltec training was invaluable. Swami expected us to handle our minds and take responsibility for our internal world. This was the beginning level of spirituality. He expected us to take care of it.

I learned two things from this practice. First, everyone is responsible for their own happiness. Second, never take things personally. Both practices served me well. An example, if Swami said hello when you walked by, that was nice, if he didn't, that was fine, too. I didn't have any expectations about him interacting with me and didn't take it personally if he didn't. I think Swami was happy about that. The other side of that, if Swami was busy or having a hard day and would nip at me a little, I didn't take that personally either. I didn't take that in. However, a lot of people did. That was a big learning, whatever Swami said, to not go up and down with it. Trust in your own experience. Trust in yourself.

It seems that a lot of students didn't have prior spiritual training to deal with their mind and internal reactions. I noticed that students who had been involved with another popular form of meditation, could meditate but didn't seem to have tools to deal with their minds. They could get energy but were unbalanced emotionally and hadn't developed self-reflection.

Swami was working on people's fears and insecurities, bringing them up to purify them, and he was *really* good at it. But people could easily spin out in their minds, seeing it in a negative way. Swami's teaching to handle those thoughts was to just throw them out. That sounds great, but it takes a person who knows how to control their mind to do that.

The thing was, Swami was not teaching the ABC's, he was teaching the Ph.D. level. His dharma was to give out the knowledge. He knew his lifespan was short; he couldn't focus on beginning level spiritual things. Historically, to be eligible for these advanced practices you had to have been purified and able to handle your mind, and have control of your reactivity. For sure, when you're around an avadhut, you will turn to ash if you don't figure it out. If you can't dissociate yourself from your mind, it is just going to eat you up.

Sivapriya: And the Toltec work that you did taught how to recognize what was even happening, that you were in a reaction to the past. Then you could say, 'Oh, that's touching a nerve of some old energy that's not healed.'

Terry: Yes. If you practice it, it's not so hard. But when you first start it's overwhelming, because you have so many reaction points. Most human beings are covered with emotional wounds, as if we have sores all over our body. We are comfortable with other people that have had the same wounding, so they become our friends, and we have these silent agreements not to touch those wounds. We come to think it's normal to be covered in these wounds and to work around them. The approach to take is to pay attention to what would trigger us during the day and then to address that through recapitulation at night. It takes dedicated effort for years because many of the emotional wounds are deep. It just takes practicing and commitment.

I feel this is what Swami was asking us to do when he asked us to handle our blocks, and with all the ways he teased and tested me, he was pointing out those unhealed wounds. Sometimes you can trace it back, sometimes you can't, but even just recognizing and seeing that I'm reacting in a disproportionate way to what was said. What's behind that? Why do I have such a strong reaction to such an innocent thing, and then having the discipline to go back and see what that is touching in me that I still have a huge amount of unsettled energy around it.

Sivapriya: Did you ever feel like you reached a point where you crossed a threshold where you don't have to put quite so much energy into that?

Terry: Yes, it is self-generating. When you start doing it more, it gets easier and goes faster. Once you practice you can do it faster. You get to a point where the big ones are cleaned up, and then it is more maintenance.

Sivapriya: You saw Swami had to deal with it too, he had the human reactions that he had to handle?

Terry: Yes. Generally, they weren't huge, but he still had those disappointments that he had to handle.

Sivapriya: So, to be part of Swami's Ph.D. program, it's our responsibility to go back and take any "remedial" coursework we need to keep up!

Terry: To have a true spiritual life you need to go through the steps. How do you want to do that or which tools really work for you, that is individual, depending on what you're attracted to. What type of work do you want to do? For me, I wouldn't say it was hard. But it took awareness and consistency. Once I started to practice, I felt such a huge shift in my energy, it was inspiring. It made a huge difference in the way I felt and my outlook towards the world and not being a victim. If you have done it, then you know, you just feel better.

Another angle was, when I started practicing this, the people around me changed dramatically. Some of the people I was closest to did not like me changing. As you do this, you also start to know who is helping bring out the best in you or who is tearing you down, expecting you to stay in your wounds so they can stay in theirs. You will naturally evolve the relationships that are helping, and some other ones will fall away. Once I started, I was shocked how I changed energetically.

Sivapriya: So, you got some negative reactions from people around you, but that was actually a sign that you were healing! By the time you got to Swami, you had a good start. You got the biggest mirror of all into all the parts of yourself you didn't want to see. But you said you never felt judged by him, even when he was saying things that seem unkind, like calling you a failure.

Terry: You know, that was something I've tried to say about Swami. That's one part that made it easier to be around him. He was pointing it out but not judging you for it. He was showing it, not judging it. We could judge ourselves, but he didn't judge us. If what he showed caused you to go off, which it often did in people, he'll put them at a little distance. He was giving time to figure it out, then if you did, he would bring you back closer. And having some distance could be a good thing, because Swami could be like gasoline to those wounds. If you had anger or any emotion, he just amplified it.

Whatever comes up, it's not pleasant to see in yourself. Mostly it's everything you want to hide. 'Oh, I'm not like that!' Your ego believes you're either the worst person in the world or you're the best, and there's no in-between. We are in the middle somewhere, doing some good things and some things that aren't so good. Whether it's intentional or not, we all do things that affect other people.

Some of the times when we do things that other people have a negative reaction to, it's because of their wounds; they misinterpret what we say because of them, just like we could do with Swami. The main practice is to not take things personally. If you have good intentions, and you say something to someone and they react defensively, it could be their internal dialogue. If you meditate or do japa, you can slow the mind down. Then you can start to hear your own mind's dialogue and see if you are believing it! You can change what it repeats to be more positive, but those things are all kind of tied together. I think most people don't even realize they are separate from their thoughts. If you don't dissociate from your thoughts, your thought are the reality for you. My experience, and what Swami tried to teach us is, that's not the reality. That dialogue is what tells you everyone and anyone else is to blame!

One of the biggest things to understand with recapitulation is you are not re-experiencing it, you are just witnessing it. For example, think of a time that you said something to someone and got a big reaction from them, then you reacted back. If you practice recapitulation, you can go back as an external witness to observe that event from a neutral place. From that place, you can see that there are other options. Maybe that person was just having a bad day and what they said had nothing to do with you at all, and because you escalated it, you turned it into a huge thing instead of just letting them be in a bad mood. And you could just drop it right there. Or maybe they're pointing something out in you that you haven't been able to see, and if you just accept that, receive that reflection, then you can heal. There are a lot of possibilities. Even if you can see that in that moment there were options, you could have done something differently. No one can do that for us. You have to do that for yourself.

The last part of that process is forgiveness for yourself and for that person. One of the key things is forgiving the other person. You're not forgiving them because they deserve it, necessarily. You're forgiving them to help yourself. You're the one that suffers by not forgiving because you're holding that negativity and grudge and carrying it through time and it's affecting you.

You can feel it in your body when you let it go. There's a tension that will release. You can check because you can think about that situation and that tension doesn't come back. So that is why Swami would circle back around weeks or months later, to give me the chance to check if it was really gone! He would throw something out to see if I reacted. And, you know, like I said with him, it didn't even have to be much of a reaction, it could be subtle or energetic and he would know.

He could tell if you hadn't let go of it yet. There's no hiding from the master.

Often, Swami would call a group of students he was working with to meet with him. They would sit with him in his office or his living room. Usually, I would sit in the other room where Swami couldn't see me. Partially I did this if his family or one of the Indian staff called and I had to answer the phone. It was easier to answer the phone if I wasn't in the same room as him. The other reason was, I was around him every day. The other students didn't get to be around him like that, so I felt it should be more for them. Another part, I knew if he wanted to do anything with me, if he wanted to push me in any direction or put his attention on me, I was around all the time. I was a fish in a barrel; there was no escape for me. So, there was no use needlessly putting myself in front of him. Besides, I didn't have to. It seemed that no matter where I was, he knew exactly what I was feeling. He didn't need to be obvious. He knew what I was thinking and experiencing even if I was in the other room.

Sometimes Swami did call me to his office to speak to me personally. I always found this a little traumatic, especially if he told me to sit down. My response was, "Uh-oh, I am in the hot spot." Especially if he sat down and somebody else was serving us, then I would really be worried. It's not that easy to have the master as a mirror reflecting things you don't want to see.

Shirdi Baba Murthi, Penukonda

Inner Secrecies of the Heart

If you start to talk with your open heart, with your pure heart, then automatically the doors of heaven open. Opening the doors of heaven means opening your heart. Then you can see the reality of God, the real energy of God. He's a great loving person.

-Sri Kaleshwar

All the processes we do are fueled by the heart. The bottom line, you won't go anywhere if your heart's not open. You can't heal anyone, you can't help anyone, you can barely help yourself if you don't have an open heart. The avadhut energy requires it.

You must *want* to have an open heart. You have to practice. You must recognize when you are just going through the motions, you're not in the place you want to be, your heart is not as open as it could be. Even if you can't open your heart to many people, open your heart to one, and live in that experience with one person, that can be enough to change your world. It is enough.

There's a famous story about two guys walking down the road. There's a contest between the wind and the sun about who can get the other to take his coat off first. The wind blows super hard, what does the other man do? He pulls his coat tighter. What does the sun do? It shines and warms the other guy, so he takes his coat off! He has to! An open heart is like the sun, it melts the heart automatically.

My experience is that my inspiration goes up with my open heart, goes down when my heart closes. Swami would tell us we had to maintain our inspiration, but my inspiration was there when I was open to what was happening. This is my observation of what successful students have. It takes knowledge, but it takes more than that; inspiration and an open heart have to be there too. You need all these qualities, and surrender. If you have an open heart and surrender, you can't lose. Then you don't take things personally, no matter what happens. 'Ok, I am doing the best I can, I am trying.' If you're really feeling that, there's a huge protection.

Winning the Master's Heart

There is a saying, 'If a holy saint really loves you, if they give you shaktipat, there's a chance they can bring you what you really want. They can bring you one or two steps up if you can handle them very delicately and hook their heart in your hands, being careful not to try to 'grab' them with your hands. Just win their heart, that's it.' From there, they can start to bring you to Mother Divine. Use any channel if a divine soul is ready to help you. But you can't convince them that easily. It's a little hard. You have to show your pure love. Pure love, what is that? It's completely the deeper inner feelings of how you give your love to them. You have to develop that status from the beginning. It's called SharaNāgati tattva. SharaNāgati tattva means completely surrendering to the master.

-Sri Kaleshwar

To win the master's heart, your heart must be open. Swami often talked about having an open heart. There is hardly a talk that he didn't bring that up. But how do you do that? It's easy when you think you are getting what you want, as opposed to doing it because it's what needs to be done. If you think it should look a certain way, or want it to look a certain way but doesn't, can you keep your heart open? All of us who were closely around Swami – and I think this was unanimous – agreed none of it looked like anyone expected it would. You could resist, or leave, or get upset, but it didn't change what he was doing. Later, he had less tolerance towards any resistance. Maybe it was because he knew he had run out of time. And, how many times could he say the same thing and see his students were not understanding?

To me, an open heart to the master is the key. You can't do any of the rest of the processes, they won't work. People blame the master because they don't get results, but truthfully their hearts are not open.

Swami fueled that in people. They would have great expectations and ideas of how things would look, without seeing that you had to do something. He wasn't just handing something to you if you gave some money or showed up at a program and went through the course. You had to do the work.

One time I spoke with Ramakrishna, who told me about when he felt he won Swami's heart. Swami had said during a class that he wanted some yantras done. He came out and everyone else was gone, except Ramakrishna was there drawing yantras. He was just doing what Swami had asked, but no one else was. It isn't that hard, but you have to actually do something. If you do something, you can win. That was the surprise, it didn't take years of meditation or a huge process, but it took doing what Swami had asked.

I won Swami's heart because he told me that when he asked me to promise to take care of him for the rest of his life. Even now, I don't know exactly what I did, I just have some ideas. When Swami told me that I had won his heart, I was a little surprised. I didn't feel that I had done anything exceptional. It didn't seem that hard, but what exactly did I do? Later, thinking about it, I realized that meditating and doing the practices he taught was something. I didn't do everything he taught, but I really tried to do what I could.

He was happy that I was reading the *Mahabharata*. He was teaching about it, and I didn't know anything about it, so I read an abridged version. It was enough to get familiar with the stories. At least I knew what he was referring to and understood some basic things. Normally when he talked in public to Westerners, he would be talking to a lot of blank faces when he shared Indian stories. He gave an example, but they didn't know the stories he was referring to. It changed for me when I read some and had some understanding of his examples. Although he didn't say to read it, I felt I needed some cultural reference and understanding so I could understand better what he was trying to teach us.

You don't have to do that much to win the master's heart. It's not really that hard, but to grow and develop *that* is the real process. That is harder. It has its own ebb and flow. Part of it is timing and being in the right place. The master has to be in the right place and the student has to be in the right place, and then things will happen on their own without having to do anything. The 'right place' means the right place in the heart. It has to be genuine; it can't be with an impure heart. The way you win is by sincerely doing things. Swami was consistent in that. He could feel the underlying reason why a person was doing something; he could see the energy and tell if they were just doing it to win brownie points or if they were doing it because they really wanted to.

Another angle to understand winning the master's heart is to accept what he offers. One time a man came soliciting Swami for a donation. It was an older Indian gentleman who was doing some charitable things. Swami asked me to get his checkbook. Of course, I had to bring him a pen too. Swami wrote the check, gave it to the man, and said he could have the pen. The man said no, he had his own pen, not understanding he was getting a gift. Swami said it again, take the pen. The second time he took it.

He didn't understand that Swami was giving him a gift. I couldn't say anything, but wanted to say, "Don't be stupid, take the pen. If Swami is offering something, anything, take it!" How many things does God offer us that we are not receiving?

You Can Wrestle with the Master

If you have the master's heart, then you can start to wrestle with him. If he dings you, you can ding him back! An example of this was when Swami complained that I hadn't put any new songs in his iTunes.

I said, "No, you have 4,000 songs, and you've only listened to 1,000 of them." You don't roll over. You know what you know, you know what you are doing. If you are in that position, you can throw something back at the master. Don't say it unkindly, but say things how they are. If you are right and you know that you are right, it didn't upset him.

Swami's thing was, he wanted masters; he didn't want students. If you just roll over, even with him, you are not a master. But you better be right! Not from anger and not cowering. You have to be right, and you have to say it in a way that is non-attacking, but you can clearly state your case.

One day, Swami asked me if I would be willing to give up something for the rest of my life for God for a *Kalachakra process*. For example, something you are attached to like coffee or chocolate. I looked at him and said, "I think I already did that! I gave up my job, my life, my savings, everything." To give up a food item seemed trivial compared to what I was doing. He already got everything, all my time, my awareness, dedication. Compared to that, what was a single item? But, of course, I said, "If you want me to, I can do that." He didn't say anything.

For me, saying you are giving everything and doing it are different things. I was doing it; I wasn't just talking about it. It wasn't a theory. I was a living example. He asked in a way that was quite soft, the way he said it was a little unusual.

You have to be very aware when talking to an avadhut. When he asked me, I was clear; I wasn't disrespectful. I was honest about how I felt.

Surrender

It's hard to understand God's drama. If I go this way, He goes that way. If I go that way, He goes this way. The only solution is to surrender, 'Do whatever you want.' If you surrender, He can't do anything. Then there's no way to create illusions on us, to play games on us. Who totally surrenders to God is a pure crystal. Then definitely God is using that person's soul to do His works.

-Sri Kaleshwar

Swami gave the example of being in the middle of the ocean – everywhere you look, it looks the same. Which way do you swim? Without a Guru you are lost. What the Guru does, one day they say swim this way, the next day they say swim that way. You need to swim where they tell you even if it makes no sense. If you don't have any reference, how can you protest? If you are smart, you won't protest. If you are dumb, you will complain, 'You are making me do this for your own fun, it makes no sense, why are you doing this?' It doesn't matter why. Only the guru knows where you are going.

I was having a problem with half of my face going numb. It was disturbing; I would touch my face and it was numb! Of course, I looked it up online and read about all the terrible things it could be. So I asked Costanza about it. She said it could be something serious and recommended I go get it checked out. A day or two went by and I had an opportunity to ask Swami. I told him about my face going numb and the doctor's recommendation to get it checked because it could be something serious. I said, "I would like to go to the doctor in Bangalore to have it checked."

Swami said no. I was shocked. He said, "What's wrong with you? Stop thinking about it! Just stop thinking about it." I said ok.

I stopped thinking about it and it went away. It never came back. That's been my experience with surrender.

He says swim, you swim, he says stop, you stop. You don't ask how far or how hard, you just swim. If you don't trust him, you will have fear. He is watching and doesn't have to be around to watch you. There is no hiding from the master. He can soul travel, he has angels – he is watching you. The problem is not that you do funny stuff. We were raised in a rakshasa world, of course, we are weird. He doesn't have judgement about that, we do. If you do things and you feel bad about them, it's a problem. If you do things and you don't feel bad about them, it's not a problem. We don't need to be embarrassed or hide who we are. 'This is the way I am.' In that, there is freedom. And where are we going? We are going towards freedom, true freedom.

Swami said he was looking forward to the day when we would walk beside him.

The Western Entitlement Disease

Students want things from the master. They want enlightenment, they want healing abilities, and in Swami's case, they want miracle experiences. They come to receive, not to give.

Swami was unique in the history of spiritual masters. There is no master that has given students the kind of miracle experiences he has. His students experienced many miracles, for example, having darshan of Mother Divine and darshan of Jesus. He said it was important for everyone to experience what they couldn't believe with their own eyes.

Instead of being satisfied and grateful for these experiences, there are those who expected more. 'I had that experience yesterday, but what are you going to do for me today?' It was purely entitlement and lack of gratitude. That really killed Swami's inspiration.

During one large program, two students became upset that they didn't receive what newer students had received and complained publicly. Swami said privately that it would take lifetimes for them to receive what they asked for. They were young souls and weren't eligible for it, but it was in their soul bank accounts. But they expected it in their hands now. Swami couldn't tell them they were ineligible. Some of the fruits of your sadhana you will get now, others will come later. That's why we need patience.

Some people had darshan and could only see Mother Divine's toe. They couldn't see the whole form of Mother. Why would that be? Maybe their soul wasn't ready yet. I know some people couldn't see Her whole form. It takes soul capacity. You have to do the work. You have to get 'cooked' to develop your soul capacity. You have to do the sadhana. Your soul has to be charged with energy, and your consciousness has to rise to be eligible in the divine energy. A big part of it is purification. Your mind has to be clear enough, and you have to have silence. That can take years or lifetimes to develop.

The master has to feel that you can handle what he is giving, and you are qualified to receive it. Entitlement and ingratitude never win the master's heart or demonstrate your eligibility. A student has to have confidence in the master, but the master has to have more confidence in them. If he didn't have confidence in you, he couldn't give. It's not one way; it's a two-way street.

For example, if the master gives you something to do and you don't do it, that destroys his confidence in you. He will wait, then give you something else to do and watch to see if you do it. You must show that you are open-hearted and willing to receive whatever he gives or doesn't give. If that attitude isn't there, he will make you wait until it is.

I watched students come to him with a demanding energy. As soon as you demand anything from an avadhut, you are done, forget it. If you go off on a hard angle and think that you can browbeat him to get what you want out of him, you will never win. People would do that with Swami, and it never worked. But you could always win if you had an open heart and were humble. Even if you made a mistake, you could win him again with an open-hearted and humble attitude.

The truth is, with the right student, automatically the master will give. When a student is open-hearted and comes to them, they can't help but give. When the right person comes, whether the master wants to or not, the energy causes him to give.

The other side is, if you do something inappropriate you are put on the waiting list until you have more awareness of yourself. What I saw many times in Penukonda was people could have his trust, but then would lose it. You ask an inappropriate question, you act funny when the energy goes high, or you don't have control over your emotional reactions. He would just put them on the waiting list. Most of the time, I don't think they had an awareness of what they had done.

Some would blame Swami, saying he had promised this or that and it wasn't happening. They didn't take any responsibility. They never thought it could have anything to do with their own actions or expectations. They didn't take responsibility for themselves, they just expected him to give. That was a big thing that would run around him.

He wanted students to be inspired about what was possible to achieve, but to get there would take real dedication and serious effort. Sometimes people didn't see that; they didn't see what was required from their side. If you are dedicated, with grace you can achieve it. It doesn't mean it will happen tomorrow or next week. He said he was a shortcut master, but some people expected they would get it in six months without any effort. It took Baba 18 years to realize what the *brick* was, and you believe you will get it all in one year? It's like, you need some perspective.

I saw that those who were successful with Swami were sensitive to his energy. The student has to be sensitive to the master. He is always sensitive to you whether it appears that way or not. As a master, he is responsible for our karmas, if he gives you something then he pays a price for that. If you approach him the right way, if you are open-hearted, flexible, and not having big expectations, and have faith that he will give when it's the right time, you are not worried about it; you have the right attitude to receive what the master has to give.

The other part is, he can give it, but you won't hold onto it. Swami talked about how it was easy for women to win, but harder for them to hold onto it. With men, it's harder to win but if they get it, it's easier to hold onto.

Rakshasas ask for boons and get them. But without love, you can't reach higher levels; the boons won't last. Again and again, there are stories of rakshasas getting boons but not being able to hold on to them. Once Swami told me that another student who was on duty had collected his hair out of his bathroom. He asked me if I had done that. I said, "No, I didn't have permission. If I need that, I know you will give it to me." If he is who I believe, he will take care of me. I don't need to steal things from him!

At the end of his life, an unfortunate incident happened with some visiting Japanese students that illustrates this very well. Swami kicked them out in the middle of the night! One person in the group had been told he would get something special. Swami didn't give that but gave so much more. The person complained to the group leader about it and the group leader brought it to Swami.

Swami was upset. I tried my best to minimize it, but it just kept escalating. They wanted to see Swami, they wanted to talk to him and negotiate. He wouldn't see them, he said, "We're done, they have to go." Swami had them pack up and leave the ashram in the early morning hours. The group leaders did not recognize what caused Swami to react this way. It was something you never wanted to happen.

With the master, your attitude is number one; if you have the right attitude the energy will flow. Always that was number one. If you had aggressive energy, expectations, or irritation, he would reflect that to you.

Consistently, I saw that any diksha Swami gave, someone would always argue with it! For example, if you had to be vegetarian or not have alcohol for the 41 days of the practice. They would try to get it to be more flexible. My feeling was, it is a 41-day process, it's not a big deal. It's not the rest of your life! Don't negotiate it down. It's your protection. I couldn't believe that people didn't understand that or thought they could negotiate with Swami to make it easier and somehow it would be better! If you are worried, you should err on the side of being too strict rather than not strict enough. Dikshas are protection. You have to give up something to get something. They wanted to have divine experiences, but weren't willing to sacrifice some comforts.

Truthfully, I didn't have much tolerance for the people who complained when they were at the ashram. One student complained, "I have been here for 6 months." Their point was it was a long time, and they hadn't yet received what they expected. I said, "So you're greater than *Paramahamsa*, greater than Baba? Do you think you should go faster than them? Your priorities are a little off." I was running around doing a million things and she was whining about being there for six months? What does a shortcut mean? It took Baba 18 years to realize what he had received from his master, ten years to figure out how to operate the brick he was given. What is a shortcut? Five years? Ten years? Twenty? It's not six months. That is the Western entitlement disease.

Swami said many times that Indian saints dedicated their whole lives to meditation. Even with that, they didn't experience darshan at all, or only when they died! Swami was giving the super shortcuts, but Westerners didn't recognize what they were getting. This student was in the group that birthed

Atma lingams. They received a huge amount but didn't appreciate it. There's a period of digestion after you receive the energy in a process, it takes time. I think that is why he told everyone to read the stories of saints' lives. This helps to get a realistic understanding of what you are asking for and what the saints had to go through. That helps to create gratitude for what you are receiving, rather than entitlement.

Disturbing an Avadhut

The Guru, it is said, can save from the wrath of Shiva, but none can save from the wrath of the Guru. Attached to this greatness there is, however, responsibility; for the sins of the disciple recoil upon him.

-Mahanirvana Tantra

Avadhuts are vessels of cosmic energy. They generate the highest spiritual energy on the planet, that is their dharma. It is important to understand that they are carrying that energy and how that energy reacts in nature and on you. You must be aware of the power and sensitivity of that energy and be in service of it.

My intention was to take care of his environment, to minimize Swami's stress and create a peaceful atmosphere. This was so he could focus on the big things. Sometimes I made some mistakes. Inadvertently, I did some things that impacted him badly.

One time I was on duty when Swami told me not to let anyone disturb him. Nityanandaji was giving him some medical assistance. I had closed the door to the temple, but didn't lock it since people didn't come without permission. I was filling the oil on the altar lamps when I heard loud banging on Swami's door. Someone had walked by me, and I hadn't heard them! It was Swami's good friend, Suri, banging on the door. It interrupted Nityanandaji's procedure, and it was really painful for Swami. He was so upset he came out of the door yelling! So, I got a three-day vacation.

The thing about being sent away was, he did it for my benefit, to protect me. When you hurt an avadhut, any divine being, the energy will reflect on you negatively. It happens automatically because of the protection circles around them. Even inadvertently, doing something against them will make that energy come back on you very quickly.

The next morning someone came and told me, "Don't go to the Mandir, don't be seen by Swami. You can get food but go immediately back to your room. Don't let him see you." I had watched him take that approach with people before. It was a risk; if he saw me, or thought about me, that energy would reflect on me. I said, "Ok! no problem! I will stay in my room!" It was not a punishment; it was for my protection.

I had seen someone get frustrated with Swami and throw a pen at him. Swami didn't react, he didn't even seem to notice it. But when that person walked out of the Mandir, they tripped and fell into a ditch! That is the karma of doing something harmful to a divine soul. If you approach with any aggression or harmful intent, it is very dangerous. That energy will return to you. This happens without any intention on his part. It can happen quickly. You have to be impeccable in managing your energy around divine beings.

After that mistake, the door was always locked in the Jesus Temple. Anyone who wanted to come in had to call me to open the door. If there is a chance for Maya, it will come. That was the lesson I learned. Next time, be more alert, and never make the same mistake twice around him.

A big mistake to make around an avadhut is to disturb their energy. One time I did this by going against my intuition and giving in to pressure from others. Some attendants wanted to ask Swami about a big leela running in the ashram. The leela involved a young female student who had become fixated that she was going to marry Swami! She started buying red roses and giving them to him every time she visited. In the Indian tradition, you only give red roses to your wife or your husband. Swami wouldn't even allow the flowers to come upstairs. We would give them away. The student was asked to leave the ashram several times because of her inappropriate behavior.

My interactions with her happened when she tried to give something she had brought for Swami. The protocol was to take any gift to the office. She wouldn't do that. When I talked to her, she would ask a question, I would tell her an answer she didn't want to hear. She would turn right around and ask the next person she thought she could manipulate to get the answer she wanted. She pretended to be innocent. Certain things would show up upstairs because she kept asking people until finally someone would bring it up. Her behavior was totally inappropriate and created a lot of disturbance, but Swami's compassion always let her come back.

One time, she was about to get on a plane to come back to the ashram for a program. Some attendants wanted to ask him if it was ok for her to come back. They were making a big deal about it. Those attendants had a relationship with Swami that was different from mine. Certain things they did were totally inappropriate for me to do. I just learned that I had to follow my intuition what to do. They were going on and on about this student coming, she was getting on the plane, and they needed to know before she got on the plane if it was ok for her to come.

I was upstairs in the Jesus Temple with Swami but felt that he was unapproachable. They kept sending me more and more frantic messages that I had to find out. "We need to know, we must know, we don't want her to show up, it's going to be a huge deal." Against my better judgement, I approached him on his northeast bed. I told him these attendants were really worried about this student coming, she was about to get on a plane. I said, "If you don't want her here, now is the time." But Swami couldn't have cared less. "You interrupted my meditation. I was almost done." He didn't use a mala when he was doing japa. It was a big deal. I went against my intuition, and I paid for it, and so did Swami.

One time, there was an object on the Jesus altar that we kept finding in odd places, not on the altar. We thought the cleaning crew didn't put it back in the right place, so I and another attendant kept putting it back. Turns out, it was Swami who took it off. One day he picked it up, wound up, and threw it against the wall, super hard! He didn't want it on the altar and had kept taking it off and putting it in different places. We kept putting it back on the altar because we didn't know it was him. We had never imagined it was Swami.

It was an innocent mistake, but it had disturbed him. I apologized and said I didn't realize it was him who had taken it off. The thing with Swami was, he wouldn't tell you that he didn't want it there. We should have figured it out, been more in tune with him. After that we were more attentive.

Of course, there are also the small day-to-day mistakes of just not being able to get everything done on my list, or just naturally losing track of one of the many things he had asked me to do. Sometimes, I would get four out of five of the items on my list done and, of course, he would ask me about the fifth one. The way to handle that was with no justifications, no explanations. I would just say, "Swami, I missed that, I will take care of it now. No problem." If you were not going to own it, if you made an excuse, he would know. Better to just say right off the bat, "I forgot. I will do it right now." Blaming someone or something didn't work very well! If he was unhappy, I didn't defend or explain even if there was great reason.

Whether he asked for something and it did not get done, or something was supposed to happen and didn't, I took responsibility. If I gave an instruction to the office and they didn't follow through, it was my fault. I would never say the office didn't follow through. Swami wanted it, it didn't happen, it was my responsibility. That was my approach to winning the avadhut energy. Just accept that it is not fair, take responsibility, and don't waste his or anyone else's time with excuses and explanations.

The stance to take if you receive a harsh reflection is to accept it and look in the mirror. Do not respond with more craziness, explaining, arguing, defending, or justification. This will escalate the energy. A calm acceptance is the best, even if it doesn't seem appropriate or apply to you. Every word you say, you are just putting your foot in your mouth further.

Some students made big mistakes, yet it seemed Swami often gave them second chances. Why did he give some repeated chances? They took responsibility and learned from their actions. If you wanted to stay, you had to learn.

I made some big mistakes but I took responsibility. I acknowledged my mistake, no matter how painful it was. My mistakes were amplified because they directly impacted his life. If you just waved a white flag and didn't justify your actions, he would move on. But it had to be real surrender – your energy has to surrender.

The avadhut lives in the moment and won't hold on to anything. Swami could be extremely upset in the moment, you could feel singed, but five minutes later, he would be smiling. You might have lost some of the master's trust, but if you swallowed your pride, you could build that trust again. I knew whatever happened, he had to pay way more. If I had to pay a thousand dollars, he had to pay ten.

The Art of Buttering

At least you have to say, "Hi Swami, how are you? Everything ok with you? I'm little hungry, can you please give a banana? You have ten bananas can you give one banana to me, please?" You know, giving orders. I said the whole of the Indian tradition is buttering, it's nothing but huge buttering. Then finally, 'I want that, give it to me.' Not going straightly, I want that.

-Sri Kaleshwar

Swami said if you want to attract God's attention, butter on God. It's a real mechanism that is understood very well in India. All the *stotrams*, hymns, mantras, and prayers are praising God. To us Westerners, it seems so over the top when you read what they're saying! The *Hanuman Chalisa* goes on and on about every detail of how wonderful Hanuman is: his earrings, his hair, everything! In the *Baba Stotram*, it says, you're the greatest, you control everything, you are everything. It really is a mechanism. You must get their attention and get them feeling good, so they'll give you something! They say God comes if you praise God with sincerity. People hear, 'I must chant this,' but not that you must chant it with an open heart. Maybe it will partially work, but if you do it with longing, that's the key. You must do it with sincerity.

An example of that mechanism applied to complimenting Swami. If you gave him a sincere compliment at the right time, he would respond in a beautiful way; you could hook him with that. Swami said the same thing about God. You have to be complimentary in a real way. It's an art. Do it sincerely, then God will respond. Swami said God would just give certain things away if you know how and when to ask. If you know the mechanism, then you can use it to your advantage. But you have to understand it is a soul mechanism, that's what makes it so effective. So, if you butter on a divine soul, you will get divine things, but you have to practice. If you did it sincerely, Swami would respond. It's the same with God.

Satsang: A Buttering Channel

Terry and Sivapriya, Virtual Ashram, 2021

Sivapriya: So, buttering on the master, and on God, or actually really on anyone, is one way to win their hearts if you do it right?

Terry: Yes. Swami made that term up and joked about it. But when it comes down to it, I don't know how many people actually understood it. He would say that he had that "buttering channel" as one of the ways to communicate to pull the Mother!

Sivapriya: That sounds important! But he would use it in other ways too, not just with God, he would butter on people too, right?

Terry: He could open people's hearts that way, and no matter what he asked, you couldn't say no to him! He knew what he was doing.

Sivapriya: Well, having observed you out in the world, I see that you implement buttering almost everywhere you go. I mean, I've seen you do it with checkout clerks and receptionists, and just about everyone you interact with. I am guessing that is not an accident.

Terry: Practicing on salesclerks, yes, that's an attempt to exercise that same thing. And it works. But you can also do it on a bigger scale.

Sivapriya: Well, doing it on a salesclerk is one thing, there is a soul and a heart there and something is happening. But doing it with an avadhut or a really charged soul, a divine soul, is another. If you generate that kind of positivity in anyone in our Sai family, you can access real power!

Terry: First is to understand the mechanism, and then to practice it and be able to use it. As a healer, you need the person to be open, if you can do that. It's not coercion, but they need to be open. You need to be able to do that, to open someone.

Sivapriya: Yes, in a recent transcript we studied in Nityanandaji's classroom, Swami made it clear that as healers and teachers we can't work with anyone whose heart isn't open. So, it's a skill we need as Sai Shakti healers. From what I observe you doing, you meet people where they are, and pay attention to them. Listening and observing doesn't take much. But still, sometimes you can't get through.

Terry: Swami talked about that; some coconuts are harder than others. Like when you are at an abhishek or a puja, cultivating that, if you have an open heart, if you are sincere, it changes the whole experience.

Sivapriya: Otherwise, you are just going through the motions.

Terry: Then they are just rituals, and you are not going to get the real thing, or you are just going to get two drops instead of a river.

Sivapriya: So, you feel like Swami made it clear that buttering was an important skill for us to have?

Terry: It's super important. You need to be able to engage. If you want to engage with God, in a way that is meaningful to God, you need to practice buttering. And like I said, it must be sincere. I mean, do you think you can fool God? You're going to get the opposite result! Practicing on store clerks is beginner level. You can see how to be with each person, you have to try a few angles to see what works. I have no doubt whichever deity you're talking to, it's going to be the same; you may have to work at it to get the right angle, but it's possible. There's no mistaking it when you get it, because you get back a huge rush of energy.

Swami with students at his dhuni, 2011

Developing Spiritual Masters

In one way, having had a previous guru was a boon. On the other hand, I had to unlearn a lot of things that I had learned or thought to be true. They were baggage. My process with Swami was going through a lot of unlearning. Swami complained about other gurus adding their masala, their own mix of spice, to the teachings because they wanted to keep students as students. They didn't want to teach how they got where they are, so they gave a watered-down version of the knowledge. For example, it was important to be vegetarian and celibate to be spiritual. This isn't necessary, except as a diksha for certain processes at certain times. My idea of being spiritual was to be sattvic (pure) because that's the way I had been taught. And it was my natural inclination.

Swami wanted to put an end to studentism, that the guru was up top, and the students were below him. He was radical because he wanted to change that. Of course, what he taught was advanced. He didn't spoon-feed us. He demanded we figure things out for ourselves. Unless you can figure things out for yourself, how you achieved what you did, you are not a master. To be a master means you can teach someone else to get to the same place.

Interview for Indian Television

Penukonda, 2002

Interviewer: Why did you choose to leave your life and come here?

Terry: I had been looking for a real experience in life. I had been on many spiritual paths before, but when I met Swami, he was the first teacher I met who said he could show me how to reach the point where he was. No other teacher had ever told me that before.

Interviewer: Have you been with many other gurus?

Terry: One guru and other teachers.

Interviewer: How do you find Swami different from them?

Terry: Swami is much more challenging; he pushes his students much harder than any other teacher I've had. Yet, the rewards are much greater. I've learned more in three years with Swami than many years with other teachers.

Interviewer: Can you say what his pattern of teaching is like, how is it different from others?

Terry: Swami gives more, but he asks more of me. He gives tests. He is like a schoolteacher, but much more difficult. Most teachers give, but they don't question you. Swami questions very deeply to test your understanding of what he is giving.

Interviewer: Your search for truth, was it due to some stress or any kind of difficulties in your life that you wanted to leave and come here?

Terry: No, for me, all my life I had been searching, so that is why I had many teachers right from my childhood.

Interviewer: In short, how would you differentiate your guru from other gurus?

Terry: That no other teacher had said that they could take me from where I am to where they are. Mainly they would say, here's something I can give you, to give some satisfaction. They would never say they could take you from where you are to where they are.

Interviewer: How do you differentiate your life from before you came here and after?

Terry: One of the biggest things I noticed is the stillness of my mind. The longer I am here, the slower and slower my mind goes. I have much more peace and I feel much more at home.

Interviewer: You like it?

Terry: Yes, very much.

Interviewer: In these three years, have you experienced any miracles?

Terry: Yes. I was with Swami on Christmas day. We had a wooden cross and the wooden cross bled. I was present when that took place, I felt the huge energy, the divine energy; it was really beautiful.

Interviewer: When we are talking about miracles, you will find other people who are capable of performing miracles who will not be to this spiritual level. Don't you think people who are searching for truth might be misled when they are searching for miracles?

Terry: Yes. I can say I wasn't looking for miracles, but I was looking for a teacher. Swami's love and dedication to his students really impressed me. Then afterward, he was performing miracles. I didn't come because of the miracles but I was here and was able to experience the energy with the miracles.

Interviewer: I ask this question because I want to know what is the importance of miracles in a spiritual circle?

Terry: The biggest thing is, it's a demonstration of God's energy. A real miracle you can feel very clearly inside yourself that it is divinity. There's no fooling, in your heart, you know. For me, it was very, very clear.

Interviewer: So you knew what you were seeing.

Terry: Yes. Absolutely.

Interviewer: So what was your goal when you came here and what was your ambition?

Terry: Because Swami said he could take me to the place he was, that was my goal.

Interviewer: If you reached the place you wanted to go, afterward what would be your plans?

Terry: He committed for all his students to go into the world and give to the world. So for me, to go back to the United States and to teach and to show others what Swami has shown me.

Interviewer: What would be your message to the world after your three years of experience?

Terry: What I can say is that it's real and that it is possible to receive; his students are proof of that.

Interviewer: So what do you think of the planet and the way it is going? Where is the need for the spiritual circle?

Terry: I think that clearly things in the world are getting worse, and that through spiritual experiences people can once again turn towards God and have a real experience of God in their lives.

Interviewer: Do you think a point like that will come soon?

Terry: Yes, I think that is possible as Swami's students grow and develop, we will go into the world, and we will help people who are yearning to reach God.

Interviewer: Your master told you you would become a master, now you can go anywhere in the world to spread the message. Then, what will be your feeling, have you any comments on your master, that he will prepare you as a master?

Terry: I feel very confident in the three years that I have been here that Swami has been guiding me step-by-step to become a master. I feel that I am not finished yet, I am still here, I am still working, but when the time is right, he will complete that process and I will become a master. I have no doubt about that.

Mandir

AT THE END

I'll be with you no matter what. I'll be with you no matter what. I will be with you no matter what! In any circumstances, any painful time, hard time, happy moments, any moment, the Guru Parampara is with you.

-Sri Kaleshwar

Samadhi, March 18, 2012

Samadhi, 2012

I Am Always with You

I raced motorcycles when I was a teenager. People would accelerate for a few minutes on the racetrack and feel so good, thinking they were so speedy. What they didn't realize was that on a racetrack, if you let up, in the blink of an eye, ten people pass you and you are in the back. If you don't keep pushing, everyone gets past you. It's like that with a guru, you can think, I am so great, I am so fast, but if you are with other people, suddenly you are not so fast or great the second you let up. When a real guru is there, you don't get that second to let up. You would never push yourself as hard as he can push you. If you have a guru, they will keep pushing you to do better, making you know it was just a step, a warm-up, but you thought it was the finish!

When I raced motorcycles, many people would talk about how fast they were. I was like, no problem, come to the track. You could see quickly; maybe they were fast on one section but they could not put the whole thing together or put it together for a race. You are not born with that. It takes practice. Even for people who are naturals, it takes practice and training. It's the same way on a spiritual path. Maybe you have some past life experience, your soul has some capacity, but you still have to go through it again. We just can't understand how blessed we are to have the guru's energy in our lives.

I always laugh when I think no school guidance counselor ever offered me the job option of serving an avadhut! No one prepared me for that. Swami was so incredibly magical, fun, way beyond what you could ever imagine. From the first time I met him and moved to India, to living and working around him the way I did, I got to see what a character he was. I was around him a lot. He had me do guru seva. That was his choice. Of course, I was a willing participant and knew at least some of the opportunity that was there.

I had a tourist visa and would have to leave the country every six months. After I got back from a visa jump, the first thing Swami always said to me was, "What did you get me?" He didn't need anything; he just wanted to know that I was thinking about him no matter where I was. I never went anywhere without getting him something. I started buying him little electrical things that I knew would make his life better. He wanted us to be thinking of him. He never told me that, but that's my interpretation of why he would ask me that. The stuff I bought wasn't important. I was thinking about him, that's what was important! He was training me to concentrate on him all the time, whether he was around or not, even when he was not in the body. Because, of course, he is still here. Just because he's not in the body anymore doesn't mean he's not here. Sometimes I forget, but then he is there. That was my experience being around and serving him; it didn't matter where I went; he was there.

I would be away from him physically but knew he knew whatever I did. If he asked me something about it, I would always tell him because I knew he could figure it out. He knew what I was experiencing and didn't judge me for it. He would judge you if you denied what you were experiencing or if you tried to hide it from him. 'Okay, he knows. But he still accepts me.' It made it easier to accept myself. 'Okay, he sees me as I am and it's good. He's fine with it, so why aren't I?' It helped me to come to the place of self-acceptance. I have my quirks, at least my share, but it's okay. I don't have to be my idea of a perfect person. I just need to be who I am. There's great security in that.

When I made the promise to take care of Swami, I had no idea it would be eleven years. The first few weren't so intense. The last five or six were very intense as Swami's schedule and energy got harder and harder.

Swami started staying out of the ashram more and traveling on the Full and New Moons. He was starting to disassemble his *protection circles*. Penukonda created the protection circles around him; it was his power spot.

He became more intense in his interactions with people. As time went on, Swami saw that being subtle wasn't enough, the students weren't getting it. They weren't seeing their own stuff. I think he had to become so intense because he wasn't being successful with all the students. An avadhut will go to any extreme to make you free. His students' blocks forced him to go to that extent. It was his job to point to where we are stuck, and it's our job to take care of it. After he pointed something out, you had to recognize it and change your behavior. That's doing the work. If you hide from it, it just gets bigger and bigger. If you don't take care of it when it's little, then it just keeps getting bigger and bigger. Why Swami's reactions became more intense was because people weren't recognizing themselves. If you don't, it just gets more intense. Then what's the next technique of the ego? Well, a lot of people just got better at hiding it. It didn't go away because they weren't willing to look at themselves. It's just too easy to blame it on external circumstances or other people.

At the end of Swami's life, he sent very senior students away and didn't invite them back for the rest of his life. My opinion was, it was because they weren't looking at themselves and taking responsibility for what they were doing. The avadhut energy will amplify your blocks. If you resist the process and choose to stay a victim, eventually that energy will push you away. It's a protection.

His behavior became more extreme. He kept moving further and further from the gentle person we originally met. It was hard. He was often harsh. I am not sure I would have stayed without that commitment to him. I would tell myself, 'Ok, I made a commitment. I said I would do this; I need to do it.'

Through his acting strangely, I could see he was still there. He would smile at me, and he was there. My feeling was, he had a reason that he was doing all the things he was doing, I didn't understand it, and it wasn't easy. Even then, I did what he asked me. I wasn't always enthused about it, but I tried to maintain that. I knew clearly why I was serving him. It's taken some time and distance to put it all in perspective. But I never had doubts about Swami. Never.

Swami had said all along that he wasn't going to stay for long, but the fact that he really did take off was still a shock. He was so good at creating smoke screens. But you could clearly see that he was upside down. He had gone from being awake all the time to asleep all the time. Near the end of his life, he was sleeping a lot. He had gone from being awake for 20 or 22 hours a day to a complete reversal. He would sleep almost all the time and only be awake for short periods.

During that time, he would often sleep in the Jesus Temple at Jesus' feet. That is when he wanted me around him. He wanted me to stay up there all the time. During that time, Mataji and Nityanandaji were coming and talking with him, interviewing him about Jesus. He was on his bed in front of Jesus with them sitting next to him talking. He was talking to them; their conversation was really low.

He wanted only oil lamps and all the electric lights out. There was a small divan outside his living room that I would sleep on. Sometimes I would sit up and meditate. Swami wanted me there and wanted me to be awake.

During that time, Swami would call out to me to see if I was there. Or he would say, "Is it safe?" I would say, "I am here, Swami. It's safe." Safe, meant I was there and no one else was that he didn't want. One part, he was just checking I was there, and I was awake.

He would often have me sleeping in the upstairs apartment during that time and wouldn't let me go home. I learned from Nityanandaji that Swami was taking *yoga samadhi* during that time. Swami never told me. That's how it usually was.

Before his final samadhi, he kept me up there for some days. But the night he took samadhi he sent me home. It was good that I wasn't there when Swami took samadhi. I felt that he sent me away on purpose. He had Nityanandaji with him. He always said that Nityanandaji would be the last person to see his face alive.

The first time we met him, he told us he would be taking samadhi. I thought it would be a couple of years. But ten years later when he took off, it was still a huge shock. He really did it!

Postscript

Who does sincere hard work, I'm always with them. I'm for them. I am in them. That's my word to the universe. If they're a little up and down, bumpy, I make them huge bumpy. That's my nature. If they're coming straight, I walk straight. To your actions, I'm your mirror. Whatever your face, I will show back to you. That's it.

-Sri Kaleshwar

Swami tried to teach us about avadhuts. Being an avadhut in the modern age is extremely difficult. Historically, they have kept themselves hidden. How can people possibly understand the avadhut consciousness? All gurus are not avadhuts. There are spiritual teachers who are not at that level, and those who don't have the best intentions of the students at heart and become corrupted by power.

Swami prepared us for years telling us he would become avadhut. Of course, we didn't know what that meant or looked like.

At the end of his life, he sent most everyone away, even long-time students. There weren't many of us that he wanted around. Mataji, Nityanandaji, Taylor, Ramakrishna, Patrick, and I were there and have been together here at the Divine Mother Center since his samadhi. The truth is, many students, even very close ones, reacted negatively towards him, and had doubts about him, which he fueled. He had been telling students for a few years that he was going to filter people at the end, to see who was who, and who would really stand for the truth. He did a terribly effective job at filtering. He acted wild, which fueled people's negative opinions. He deliberately dismantled most structures he had put in place in the ashram. He became extremely direct. He was a laser beam focusing directly on you. If you brought your ego and craziness, it was mirrored back amplified, and it wasn't gentle. Even if you didn't say anything, just being in the same room, Swami felt it and would reflect it to you pointedly. He was like Mahakali chopping off the ego's head with a sword!

There is a story about how *Marpa, Milarepa's* guru, treated Milarepa. Milarepa's family had an injustice done to them that made them destitute. Milarepa tried to rectify it by learning black magic to exact revenge. So, he got a boatload of karma. He recognized his mistake and searched for a master to help him rectify his karma. Marpa told him to build a house. He built it brick by brick; when it was finished, Marpa told him to knock it down. This happened nine times in nine years.

Finally, the master's wife couldn't bear the treatment this guy was getting. She intervened and stopped the 'cruelty' to his student. Marpa said, "You don't know what you just did! His karma was almost done. Now he has to start again!" Marpa was making him do something terrible, but in reality, he was clearing Milarepa's karma. Milarepa would have been done sooner if the guru's wife hadn't intervened. Compassion looks different through the guru's eyes because they can see the whole situation.

We walked into the darkest time ever, this Kali Yuga. Swami was playing with a lot of people's karmas. A lot of those have to do with the time around Jesus. A lot of his students were with Jesus. That is a big soup of karma. Can you imagine if you could see all of it?

He said we had to explain to the world why he had to do some of the things he did, why avadhuts like Baba had to smoke ganja, why Jesus drank wine. People are thinking of them, praying to them, pulling them, and they are seeing all of it in their third eye! When Swami would eat, he liked to have someone to talk to so he could eat without having that third eye interference of people who were thinking of him. Avadhuts must relax their minds from all that. It's required. It's a big problem when you are at that level and taking care of all those souls energetically, handling their karmas; you have no idea what that's like. More people in the future will be like that, they have to know how to handle the energies.

Nobody knows what it is like to be around an avadhut unless you have had the experience; to understand their energy, how they operate, how to approach and interact with them. Certain things if you do, your interaction won't end well. I want spiritual students to be able to understand. There are avadhuts in this world who live in the highest state of consciousness and knowing how to interact with that energy allows you to win their grace. This is the greatest blessing.

An avadhut is incredibly sensitive. They perceive more, they feel more. Your attitude, what you bring to the interaction, will always be reflected. You have to be careful about what you bring to them, or what you are carrying in you. You may not even know, but they will reflect it. If you bring expectations and demands, you won't get what you want. If you come with an open heart and sincerity, most likely you will get the best thing for you, probably something that you wouldn't even know to ask for.

The avadhut is the embodiment of unconditional love. They are here to take care, but you have to have an open heart and adjustable nature. People have all kinds of romantic ideas of what it was like to be around Swami. Even senior students had some real misperceptions. I want to set the record straight. I want to help students understand.

Your attitude is the number one thing; if you have the right attitude, then the energy will flow. Swami would immediately reflect back every time you had aggressive energy, expectations, irritation. If he found one spot where he would get a rise, that was the spot he went for and found all the angles to get there. After a while, you learn, you don't fight it, but just accept and surrender to it. You will figure it out. If you have any resistance, it will only get worse.

I'm getting more like Swami all the time. I saw a lot of things Swami did but didn't understand why. Now I am understanding why. Why he acted that way, why he had those kinds of reactions. Westerners thought he should be perfect, calm, and smooth and relaxed. That's not the way it is. There were moments of frustration and anxiety, normal human stuff. Wanting to give and not having people that can receive. It's like he was speaking a foreign language.

In Swami's house in Kadapa, when he would whistle for me, his parents would joke, "Are you calling your dog?" They didn't understand what he was doing. It's the master-student relationship. I didn't understand it either. But the big thing was, my heart was open. Even if he treated me poorly, or appeared that he treated me poorly, my heart stayed open. My heart stayed open to him. That meant he could continue to push me. An open heart makes all the difference. If you don't open your heart, you can't receive anything.

I was anchored to Swami. I wasn't trying to control him or get him to conform to my ideas. I was giving him a lifeline, something consistent, a safe place, a base. Then from there he could go wherever he wanted. Swami would occasionally go out from his base and travel, but he was tied to his power spot, Penukonda. The vibrations in foreign countries disturbed him. He was so sensitive. Swami had to come to America to find us, but later travel wasn't so easy on him.

Once Swami took samadhi, there were periods that my heart would open but it wasn't open most of the time. I was in grief and shock. There were certain experiences, really hard things, power struggles that happened after his samadhi that did not help shorten that process. But every one of those negative experiences helped me learn compassion. I knew that my heart was not open. I was devastated, I was depressed, hoping to recover but not knowing I would, but still having faith in Swami. He put a lot of effort into me, an enormous amount. He did not waste his time.

Swami said that after he took off it would be really hard. I never imagined it was going to be as hard as it was. Swami predicted everything that would happen after he took samadhi. He asked Mataji, Nityanandaji, Ramakrishna and I, "What if, at the end, I start having dancing girls around me at the Oberoi?" He predicted most people would go against him judging his behavior. He told us it would be the darkest time in our lives after he was gone. He said everything was going to be upside down and students would do crazy things. It would look like the ancient mission's head was on the tail and the tail was on the head. It is true, it was like that. But his words guided us, "If you can keep the flame of the mission going, the mission will stay alive and will succeed." He said we would realize what he had given to us.

There are things that Swami said and did, knowing full well it would be years before we realized what he was doing or speaking about. He wasn't doing things on a one-year plan, or even a five-year plan. He was doing things on the hundreds-of-years plan. I believe it will be a lifetime process for us to understand most of what he did. Those are some of the things that Mataji and Nityanandaji are better suited at working on and understanding. People who were close and interacted with him have a better chance of figuring that out.

He gave a lot of teaching and instructions that didn't make sense at the time. Later, as your understanding grows, the hidden meaning starts coming out. You have to get to a certain level of understanding before things make sense. At first, you won't see any relevance to it because you don't have the consciousness to use it. Throughout his life, Swami was planting seeds that we would only understand later.

Swami gave us the gift of each other and this special place, the Divine Mother Center, to continue the work he started. We don't really have a choice. We have to do this. It is our commitment to him. But why not have fun along the way? You know what's great? We're going together as a group, and it's been incredible to experience that. He developed our unity while he was in the body, and it is the reality of our dharma here at the Center. I knew Nityanandaji and Ramakrishna before I met Swami. I met Mataji a few years later. We've had long relationships and lots of divine experiences with each other, and Swami is at the core of it. It's been quite an adventure. That adventure started when I met Swami. I could never have imagined how it would eventually look. Not in a million years. He's not in a body, but we are still on that adventure. Each one of us can have that in our lives, and we all can have lots of interesting circumstances to look forward to!

A Post-Samadhi Dream

I had a dream that I was in Penukonda, in the older apartment building. It was during a program, there were a bunch of people in the hallways who were very loud. Swami was dressed in white and had a scarf on. He was walking in the hallway, and nobody could see him. He was in the middle of a bunch of people. He realized I could see him. I was going to say something to the people, like they needed to be in silence, and tell them they were wasting their energy. I was going to say something, then Swami put his finger over his lips and told me not to say anything.

It was obvious to me the reason they couldn't see him was because they were wasting their energy. They didn't have any silence. He was walking around the hallway, and I was following him. They were in a room doing a special process. Swami was very curious about what they were doing. He went in, and motioned for me to wait outside. The energy in the room attracted him. He had a mischievous look; he was enjoying seeing what his students had done. He included me with looks and non-verbal commands like he used to. It was so nice to see him again and to feel so connected. Just like no time had passed at all, just a continuation of our relationship.

Wherever your Swami is after samadhi, you can see a picture of me. Then you can sit in meditation connecting to your Swami. Who thinks on me, who really thinks on me, automatically, they get my blessing and energy. That's true. That's for sure.
-Sri Kaleshwar

The Authors

GLOSSARY

Aarthi

An act of worship consisting of the waving of lights, incense, camphor etc. before a saint or holy statue.

abhishek

Ritual holy bath. In addition to water, may be performed using rosewater, milk, curd, ghee, honey, sugar, bananas, or coconut water.

Adi Shankaracharya

An Indian saint who revitalized Hinduism and Vedantic knowledge in past millennia. He was the first to bring knowledge of the Sri Chakra yantra to this planet. He installed numerous Sri Chakras in temples across southern India, including Tirupati and Sri Sailam, which continue to bless the world today.

aghora

Spiritual practice of a certain group of ascetics involving meditating in graveyards and connecting to Shiva. They go from the negative/horrible and turn it into the positive/beautiful as in the story of Ramakrishna Paramahamsa with the Bhairavi Mata; the burned arm of a dead body was turned into sugarcane and at that moment, the Divine Mother gave darshan to him. Khandana Yoga and Dhauti Yoga, which were practiced by Shirdi Baba to wash out people's karmas, are examples of processes.

Agni

Hindu God of fire.

amrutha

Divine nectar, the nectar of immortality.

ancient knowledge

Enlightenment channels revealed by the Divine Mother and written on palm leaves revealed by Sri Kaleshwar.

Atma Lingam

An Atma Lingam is created in the body of a saint. In order to release the stone from inside his body, he releases it through his mouth. An Atma Lingam is a power object, carrying the soul energy of the saint.

avadhut

An enlightened being in the highest stage, is beyond the five elements, has gone beyond body consciousness and because of that operates outside the conventions of "normal" behavior; and has the ability to command on the creation.

Baba Stotram

The 108 names of the Divine Father, Shirdi Baba.

Badava Lingam

Powerful shiva lingam installed by Krishnadevaraya. Located in Hampi. *See Hampi.*

Balaji

Venkateswara, Kali Yugas' incarnation of Vishnu.

bhajans

Devotional songs.

Brahma Kundalini Nadi

The path in the body, enclosed by the spine, through which the Kundalini energy travels. 'Nadi' means 'channel' in Sanskrit.

brick

Shirdi Baba's primary power object, connection to his master's consciousness, used as a pillow every night to sleep.

Consciousness

A creative aspect of God-consciousness that is separate from but linked to each soul, a guardian of the soul, and its greatest well-wisher. Directs intention to the soul and implements action through sankalpam (willpower). Brahma Consciousness is developed through meditation power and by receiving the master's shaktipat. Developing Brahma

Consciousness is an essential aim in the cosmic channels. *See sankalpam, shaktipat, power channels.*

Dattatreya

The primordial guru from which all lineages ultimately arise, the incarnation of Brahma, Vishnu and Shiva in a single form. Dattatreya (also referred to as Datta) is often depicted as having three heads, symbolizing the three aspects of Creation – creation (Generator), maintenance (Operator) and destruction (Destroyer). Sri Kaleshwar calls Shirdi Baba a pure Dattatreya avatar.

decharge

To release negative energy such as irritation, stress, or depression. Decharging brings relief and balance, and implements through the Five Elements channels.

dhaba

A roadside restaurant; found throughout the Indian subcontinent.

dhoop pot

Incense pot that holds coals.

dhuni

Ceremonial firepit, often kept continuously burning.

diksha

The guidelines, rules and regulations setting boundaries to create protection circles in high-energy processes, to ensure the success of the process.

Divine Court

A group of divine souls, usually not in a physical body, who are responsible for the destiny of humanity and play an important role in guiding the souls to enlightenment.

Dwarkamai

A small building in the ashram that is Sri Kaleshwar's power spot, which he has named in honor of Shirdi Baba. It is where he gives initiation to his students to open energy channels.

Five Elements

The essential divine energy channels from which all of Creation is made: earth, fire, sky, water and air. Any soul in physical form is under their influence. Avadhuts, such as Shirdi Baba, are one with the five elements and are able to command upon them.

Gayatri

A Mother Divine mantra, created by the sage Vishvamitra, which is equal to the entire four Vedas.

Guru Purnima

Full Moon in July, most auspicious moon to connect to and receive the Master's blessings.

Hampi

350 km from Bangalore, 150 km from Penukonda, an ancient village in east-central Karnataka state, India, located on the banks of the Tungabhadra River, former capital city of the Vijayanagara Empire. At its zenith during the reign of Sri Krishnadevaraya over 500 years ago, Hampi rivaled any city on the planet as the wealthiest city on Earth. Hampi is home to many power spots, including the Virupaksha Shiva temple and the Badava Shiva Lingam.

Hanuman

Monkey god who became more powerful than his guru, Ram, by continuously chanting his name.

Hanuman Chalisa

Devotional hymn in praise of Hanuman.

Hospet

Small town near Hampi. *See Hampi.*

japa

Continuous focused repetition of mantra or prayer, a meditative technique.

jiva samadhi

A "living samadhi". A saint will enter the tomb while alive then consciously take out his soul from the body. The body will stay in perfect "living" condition for thousands of years.

Kala Chakra

Literally, the wheel of time; our soul clock; originally discovered by Buddha. Purification of the Kala Chakra leads to healing of suffering and enlightenment. It holds all of our karmas and decides when and how we experience them in a lifetime. Understanding the Kala Chakra and knowing how to implement it, we become 'a person of power', becoming possible to understand the meaning in what is happening in your life and bring anything in front of you that you need.

Kalachakra Process

Refers to an ancient body of spiritual knowledge that allows for a soul to consciously move backwards or forwards through the illusion of time. First discovered by Buddha.

Kali

A form of Mother Divine as a destroyer of negativity.

Kali Yuga

The present age, the fourth and final Yuga of this Creation cycle. The 'material age,' in which people predominantly believe the material world to be the highest reality. The Kali Yuga is the darkest of the four Yugas, an age of highest negativity and suffering, in which most humans turn away from dharma and no longer seek God. Paradoxically, it is the age when it is easiest to attain God-realization and moksha.

kama

The primordial energy of the Creation, which expresses itself as desire. In human beings, this energy is primarily sexual desire but it also finds its expression in all other desires, such as material and spiritual desires.

Lakshmi

Hindu goddess of wealth, prosperity, beauty, and power; consort of Vishnu. She is associated with "maya" (illusion). Along with Parvati and Saraswati, she forms the Tridevi of Hindu goddesses.

leela
Divine play, sport; expresses the relationship between the supreme and his devotees.

Mahabharata
Narrates the Kurukshetra War between the Kauravas and the Pāndavas.

mahasamadhi
Yogic process undertaken at the end of a saint's life to consciously take their soul from their physical body. An advanced state of samadhi consciousness.

murthi
A statue of a deity or divine soul, usually made from rock or metal; receives regular worship or pujas such as Aarthi and abhishek.

Navaratri
Hindu festival that spans over nine nights (and ten days) and is celebrated in the autumn season. There are four seasonal Navaratri, but the autumn festival called Sharada Navaratri is the most observed in honor of the divine feminine Devi (Durga), and Her victory over evil.

Nine Arrows
Shiva prayer for divine protection from negativity and illusion.

padukas
Ancient form of footwear. Used ceremonially to represent the feet of the divine deity being worshipped.

Parasurama
Incarnation of Vishnu.

Penukonda
Literally, 'great (penu) hill (konda)'; site of Sri Kaleshwar's ashram, located in southern Andhra Pradesh State, 130 km north of Bangalore. The area is defined by an ancient mountain and has been a holy power spot for thousands of years. Since ancient times, innumerable Maharshis of all traditions have visited and/or lived there. Birthplace of Mahakali, and gurusthan of Dattatreya.

personal mantra

A unique mantra that acts as a divine energy channel, linking an individual soul to God's Cosmic energy; the soul's PIN code. A personal mantra is given by the guru, and connects the soul of a student to the guru's soul. It is never told to another or said out loud. A fundamental tool, required by anyone, practicing the cosmic channels.

power object

A physical object that can act as a divine energy channel. Some power objects automatically transmit blessing energy to anyone present (with or without their doing or knowing anything), while others require a PIN code to access. They come into being in a variety of ways: occurring naturally in nature; any object blessed or manifested by Mother Divine, Shiva, an angel, or a divine soul; anything your guru gives to you; a mala used in japa meditation; an object that is worshipped with great bhakti. Power objects implement through the Five Elements' mechanisms to transmit cosmic power and shaktipat to the soul. The ancient science of power objects is fundamental to the practice of the cosmic channels.

power spot

Soul home. A mechanistic shakti-energy process connecting the soul to a power spot.

pradakshina

The rite of circumambulating in a clockwise direction an image, relic, shrine, or other sacred object.

pranam

The act of showing respect by placing one's hands together in prayer, or bowing one's head to the ground.

protection circles

In the ancient knowledge teachings, a number of things create divine energy around your soul and act as a protection; an invisible wall to resist the negative energy. Those things are: doing japa, having a power spot, power object, soul object, and soulmate, and also your personal process with your master.

pujas

Sacred ceremonies.

punjabis
Indian dress for women.

rakshasas
Soul character dominated by demon qualities. Rakshasas are powerful meditators devoted to Shiva. Though they often win Shiva's boons, rakshasas are enslaved by their blocks of egoism, greed and lust, and invariably ask Shiva for powers to dominate others but which they eventually lose.

Ramakrishna Paramahamsa
Lived 18 February 1836 to 16 August 1886. One of the most important Indian saints of modern times, revered by millions of Hindus and non-Hindus alike as a messenger of God. His teachings emphasized God-realization as the highest goal of life, love and devotion for God, the oneness of existence, and the harmony of all religions. Master of the cosmic channels. For many years, Paramahamsa had daily darshan of Mother Divine in Her form as Mahakali. His student Vivekananda was the first to bring Indian spiritual philosophy to the west in 1893.

sadhanas
Spiritual practice(s).

Sai Shakti Healing
An ancient science of soul healing transmitting pure cosmic energy to a soul through the Five Elements energy channels. When a person's soul is strengthened in this way, suffering and stuck energy from heartbreak and negative experiences are removed.

sambrani
Ceremonial incense used for pujas.

sankalpam
Willpower, intention.

satsang
Spiritual discourse or sacred gathering.

seva
Selfless service.

shakti-energy channels

Meditation processes from the ancient knowledge.

shaktipat

Transmission of shakti or spiritual energy.

Shirdi

Small town in Maharashtra State (Western India) where Shirdi Baba lived, site of his Mahasamadhi Mandir.

Shiva

Transcendent, supreme, infinite undifferentiated God-Consciousness. The seed of the Creation, God in a quiescent undifferentiated state, consort of Shakti. As a proper name, the Divine Father, the male aspect of God. Also refers to the destroyer Shiva of the Hindu Trinity.

sthita pragnata

An advanced state of consciousness, the state of equanimity, in which a person is not disturbed by any external circumstances, taking everything that comes, good or bad, equally; not being overjoyed with happiness or distressed with sorrow. Reaching that state of consciousness is a great achievement for a spiritual seeker and a great protection from the illusions, maya. This state is an important goal in the cosmic channels and is embodied by Shiva.

stotrams

Devotional, spiritual texts which are meant to be sung.

The Four Agreements

Toltec teachings by Don Miguel.

tiffins

Stainless steel stackable lunch boxes used throughout Asia.

Tirupati

City in Andhra Pradesh. Site of Sri Venkateswara (Balaji) Temple.

Venkusa

Shirdi Baba's master. Very little is known about him.

vibhuti

Sacred ash.

Vishnu Sign

Soul diagram or energetic structure of Vishnu.

Vivekananda

Lived January 12, 1863 to July 14, 1902. Disciple of Ramakrishna Paramahamsa, he traveled to America in 1893, and was the first Indian saint to introduce Indian spiritual philosophy to the West, teaching that all faiths are ultimately one and the same.

yoga samadhi

To leave the body, often for three days, soul traveling; during this time, the body appears utterly lifeless but does not decay.

INDEX

To Learn More

Divine Mother Center

The Divine Mother Center is a spiritual home for a global community of students, teachers and healers who are committed to preserving, teaching and implementing the ancient palm leaf knowledge of our spiritual lineage: Shirdi Sai Baba, Swami Kaleshwar, Jesus Christ, Ramakrishna Paramahamsa, Ramana Maharshi, and Babaji.

The Divine Mother is at the heart of the Center's mission, recognizing that She represents the feminine face of God in every culture, race, and religion. As we awaken and stand for a reverence of the Divine Mother and the sacred feminine around the globe, we connect to the feminine healing power of the Divine, birthing a higher collective consciousness. The Divine Mother Center bridges ancient spiritual technology with modern life by implementing the knowledge given to earliest peoples directly from the Divine Mother to connect with Her and making that knowledge accessible to anyone who feels called to study and practice it.

These ancient proven practices and healing techniques bring awakening of consciousness to grow and deepen our connection to Mother Divine and are available to anyone at any stage of life or spiritual practice. Through online education programs for beginning and advanced students, daily broadcasts of worship and devotion, sacred ceremonies and long-distance energy transmissions, the Divine Mother Center offers the opportunity for anyone who is ready, to awaken and develop these channels and access the wondrous, miraculous capabilities within themselves and all of Her creation.

To learn more about the Divine Mother Center, please visit us at www.DivineMotherCenter.org.

Activities of the Divine Mother Center

Virtual Ashram

The Virtual Ashram is an online gathering place for students of the Divine Mother's Ancient Palm Leaf Knowledge. The Virtual Ashram offers a growing library of living knowledge, with classes consisting of live broadcasts covering over 30 topics with multiple teachers engaging weekly with students of all ranges of experience. This online learning community is open to anyone interested in deepening their spiritual practice through live, remote learning, small group and private sessions, and a range of community engagement opportunities. Whether you're new to meditation or seeking a deeper connection with the Divine, the Virtual Ashram meets you where you are. All courses are open to anyone regardless of spiritual path, religion, or belief, and no prior meditation experience is required.

Free downloadable recordings of The Holy Womb mantras can be found as a resource on the Virtual Ashram website. Find out more at www.VirtualAshram.health, and join us as we gather together to grow and transform during this time of change!

Divine Mother School

The Divine Mother School is an online learning community of students, teachers and healers who are awakening the Divine Feminine through the teachings of the Ancient Palm leaf Knowledge. Using these ancient formulas for bringing us closer to the Divine Mother in our daily lives, The Divine Mother School offers education through one-on-one support, small group sessions and large group courses, focusing on ancient practices that promote spiritual growth and development of Divine connection through pregnancy, motherhood, parenting and family relationships, women's spirituality and more. All offerings are open to anyone regardless of religion, spiritual path or level of practice. Now is the time to awaken our lost connection to the Divine Mother to bring healing and transformation to a world in need!

To find out more about how you can connect to the Divine Mother in your life, visit us at: www.divinemotherschool.org.

Peace Fires

Peace Fires, Sacred Fire Ceremonies for World Peace, is a global movement uniting people for world peace and healing. People of all faiths, backgrounds and cultures unite every month in synchronized Sacred Fire Ceremonies for World Peace live from their homes and backyards on the Full Moons, and on the Summer Solstice and New Year's Eve for 26-Hour Virtual Global Healing Events. Together we are helping transform fear and negativity with positive energy to bring an energetic shift in consciousness for peace. Join in spirit and positive action with Peace Fires in any way that speaks to you and your traditions.

To find out more and give your message of peace, visit us at www.peacefires.org. Let there be peace on earth and love for one another.

Sai Family

A gathering place for stories, teachings and experiences of the saint, Shirdi Sai Baba, for a global community of Sai lovers. To learn more and share the joy and blessings of Shirdi Sai Baba in your life, please visit www.saifamily.org.

The Holy Womb Initiative

The Holy Womb Initiative is a group of mothers, spiritual practitioners, teachers and healers who have dedicated their lives to studying and teaching the forgotten wisdom and knowledge of the Divine Mother Energy as taught by their teacher, Sri Kaleshwar. Their mission is to bring an awakening of the power and sacredness of the Womb through all stages of life, while creating a deep and lasting connection to Mother Divine.

Through sharing the ancient knowledge, the Holy Womb Initiative serves to support women and families in all stages of life, focusing on pregnancy, motherhood, parenting, and family relationships.

They believe the world will change by recognizing and deeply connecting to the Divine Mother through the sacred power of the womb, thereby bringing cooperation, compassion and unity to a world that is desperately in need.

Find out more about the Holy Womb Initiative at
www.HolyWombInitiative.org.

Printed in Great Britain
by Amazon

26882551R00159